The Road from Home

The Road from Home

love beyond bipolar disorder

Christina Brady

Tate Publishing & *Enterprises*

The Road from Home

Published by Tate Publishing & Enterprises, LLC
127 E. Trade Center Terrace | Mustang, Oklahoma 73064 USA
1.888.361.9473 | www.tatepublishing.com

Tate Publishing is committed to excellence in the publishing industry. The company reflects the philosophy established by the founders, based on Psalm 68:11,
"The Lord gave the word and great was the company of those who published it."

Cover design by Kellie Southerland
Interior design by Chelsea Womble

Published in the United States of America

ISBN: 978-1-61739-660-1
1. Religion, Counseling
2. Religion, Christian Life, Family
11.01.12

Dedication

To James, Kristi, and Stephanie my wonderful and precious family who have shown real love and commitment to me and to each other.

I love you all so very much. I leave you with this verse found in Psalm 33:20–22.

> We wait in hope for the Lord; he is our help and our shield. In him our hearts rejoice, for we trust in his holy name. May your unfailing love rest upon us, O Lord, even as we put our hope in you.

Acknowledgments

I wish to thank all those people who have supported me through the task of writing my autobiography:

To Heidi Kogut, who gave me the first thoughts and inspiration of accomplishing such a task.

To my praying family, friends, editors, thank you for giving sacrificially of your time and talent. A special thanks to my pastor, Dr. Mark Estep, for his support in writing my first book. His encouraging sermons have pointed me to God's truth. Thank you all for being examples of how we are all supposed to walk before the Lord.

To my parents, whose gracious and quiet spirit has always lived the life to look up from whence cometh my help.

To my belated husband, James, our three children, and their mates—whom we have loved from the very start.

To my Lord Jesus Christ, who makes my story valid through my secure and loving relationship in Him and Him alone.

Table of Contents

When I first met James Brady, I didn't like him. I was very wary of him, due to my misunderstanding and lack of appreciation of his intense listening skills coupled with his ability to analyze the conversation and its complexity before venturing a comment on the subject discussed. It was not long, however, before we became very close friends and I learned to value highly his analytical mind.

James did have a profound impact on me and changed my life's direction with just three short words. However, before I reveal those three short words, a story I had either read or heard almost fifty years ago is complimentary as to how James helped me through an extremely devastating period of betrayal of my supposedly mentor, business partner, and best friend.

Early one summer a twelve to thirteen-year-old young lad I'll call Chris desired to improve his physical appearance by adding as much muscle as he could. He questioned his mother on her thoughts as to how best to obtain the look of a Jr. Mr. Atlas, and she replied that he should talk to his favorite Aunt Sarah down the street. So Chris posed the same question about how to build muscle to his Aunt Sarah. Now Aunt Sarah had in her yard several stacks of old wood egg crates, wooden pallets, and several huge fallen dead trees. She told Chris to take the single blade hand saw and begin to cut up all the crates, pallets, and trees into small pieces to use in her wood stove. Chris was informed that the sound of the saw blade would be soothing to Aunt Sarah and would help her to think upon his muscle-building problem. Each day Chris would cut, chop, saw, and stack the wood for Aunt Sarah while she contemplated the problem in her rocking chair. Toward summer's end, Chris finally took notice that he had gained several pounds, and it was all muscle. When Chris told Aunt Sarah what had happened, she just smiled and didn't say a word.

I called James as soon as I had discovered the total betrayal and lies of my best friend and business partner. I must have talked for nearly two straight hours expressing my hurt, anger, frustration, and fear of what all this would mean for my future. James never said a word during my verbal rampage. When I finally finished talking, I really hoped James had some words of encouragement, some idea of a course of action I should pursue, or something that would just make sense of the whole mess. His exact words to me were "Ever read Psalms?" Days later, I called to tell him what I had discovered, what he already knew.

I sure miss my buddy James.

—Glen Cook

The future is what we make of it; the past is what makes us. Although my father suffered with the label of Bipolar or Manic depression, he was still my father. I often questioned, and even sometimes continue to question, why our heavenly Father would have me go through the many struggles that I did. As the years go on, I find myself truly blessed to have had the experiences as a young child and through adolescents into adulthood. God is a loving Father and only wants what is best for us, we are his children, and he cries when we cry, and for this I can be grateful for all that he has blessed me with. Yes, blessed.

My father suffered from a clinical disability, but many of us suffer from something larger than life itself, a loveless life. My father left me with many questions, but he also left behind a woman who holds steadfast to what she knows to be true in her heart. That God above is always there to lend an ear or a shoulder to lean on.

I know the path of life is not easy for anyone to go through, and I am not stating or trying to state that my life experiences have one of greater severity than others, but I can say that the reason I am who I am is because of what I had the opportunity to experience.

"Kristi, life will not be easy, but always remember that God is always there," my father used this quote many times while I was a child. I ran from it until I understood the importance and simplicity of what "always there" meant.

Although there was abuse, as you will read over the chapters it would be very easy to point the fingers and blame my father for it all. I have learned to turn the negative experiences into positives by praying about it. Without the power of prayer, I know that I would not have been able to see the positives that allowed me to forgive my father.

There were many times I would cry myself to sleep with so many unanswered questions, but the most dominant one was "why?" I have found it is not the "why," but the "how" we get through the hard times in life.

If I can leave you with anything: Trust in God, for He knows, He understands, He loves.

—Kristi Brady Yetter

The beginning of mine and my husband's nearly thirty years of marriage was at times an illumination of blissfulness where I believe the angels in heaven were even coveting. His patient and kind love for me with his unselfish generosity for others, his love for God's Word, and wisdom that was given with both boldness and compassion. He had a keen sense of understanding people with such a servant's heart that no one could deny. Then there were times the effects of his erratic behavior gave terror to my emotions and tore my heart with such strong pulls of fright that it shocked the core of my inner self. With the peaks of his manic behavior I felt as if I were living with the destructive winds of a hurricane. The uncertainty of our love for each other, our finances, tomorrow's hopes and dreams; of life itself became a question I must answer. Would I be able to continue to live life like this? Is this the life of turmoil I must endure? How could I have perseverance to endure such whirlwinds of self-destruction to the person I loved so dearly? All I could imagine were the times I yearned for from my peaceful childhood.

The Road of Love

1 Corinthians 13:4–7

Love is patient, love is kind. It does not envy, it does not boast, it is not proud. It is not rude, it is not self-seeking, it is not easily angered, it keeps no record of wrongs. Love does not delight in evil but rejoices with the truth. It always protects, always trusts, always hopes, and always perseveres.

There was never any doubt about our Dad's love for each of his three daughters and son. Whether we were nut hunting, planting trees, selling his home-grown tomatoes at the roadside stand on our country road, taking yearly trips to our mom's birthplace state in Vermont, or simply making a tree fort from his left over scraps of wood, the warmth of his ever-loving heart was always securely received from his children.

It would be many years down my road before the realization of that love was indeed so rare. Dad made a living by being a carpenter. He eventually built over thirty custom-made homes and three churches throughout his life in Connecticut. He had his own sawmill, from which he cut many a timber. Mounds of sawdust from the sawed timber gave our neighbors, my brother, and me hours of playful frolicking and a mind full of wonderful childhood memories. Even to this day, when I smell cut wood, I instantly return back to my happy, good adventures, and peaceful times of childhood.

My dad's beginnings were not as joyous. His own father died when he was but two years old. His mother was left with no job and eight children, ages ranging from two to twelve. The relatives all tried to help; his Aunt Christina gave her whole paycheck over to help the widow and her family many, many times.

Ten years later, Dad decided to help his mom out by leaving home and finding his own place. He lived with a family and found a job pumping gas. He received a nickel a day plus meals. He put away every penny he had earned. By the time he was sixteen he had saved $150. He figured he would be able to buy a piece of land and build a house for his mom. She never got to see his house he and his brother were going to build because she died with her failing health at age fifty-five. Before she died she called my dad over to her bedside and asked the youngest to promise her something. With a whisper she asked him if he would always serve the Lord. As Dad kissed her forehead and choking back his tears he softly cried, "I promise." That was the beginning of his serious and genuine walk with whom he referred to so many times in his lifetime as "precious Lord."

The Road of Prayers

Colossians 1:9

For this reason, since the day we heard about you, we have not stopped praying for you and asking God to fill you with the knowledge of his will through all spiritual wisdom and understanding.

Prayer had always been a part of our family's existence. My mother's dad was a minister for many years. She always spoke of him with such love and respect. My dad once heard Grandfather Gallup pray at a camp meeting when he was very young. He referred back to that prayer a few times in his life. He knew that man had a real walk with the Lord. Later in life he met up with my mom in college. Mom would lovingly speak of dad's big, dark eyes meeting hers as he stared at her. After a few more acquaintances, Dad found out this is the daughter of the man who prayed so fervently many years before. He knew she had been brought up with God's ways. They dated a little over a year, and then he asked her to marry him. My dad of few words added, "It's either September 14, or not at all."

What could she say after he popped a question like that? They started their life on the premises that Dad, better known as Wendell Comrie, had bought in previous years for his mother. It was to be the *Comrie Homestead* on *Pumpkin Hill Road.*

Almost twelve years later, after four children Mildred, Janice, Winston, and I came along, Dad and Mom, better known as Florence, became charter members of a church. When it started, there were times when they would have prayer and fellowship right at the house. Later, when the church had bought property about twenty miles away, they would go every Sunday morning, Sunday evening, and Wednesday evening for the rest of their lives. No matter rain, snow, clouds, or sun, all six of us would always go. But I must say the most everlasting and important sermons I heard were the ones without words—lived day in and day out in our home.

We would always have our dad pray for meals and trips we took, but when it came to family quiet times together we would all participate. Not that we would have family quiet times every day, but it stands as a memory of more than just a few times. My favorite time to pray was right next to my gentle, loving dad on his knees. He always spoke with such clarity and humbleness of his heart to his precious Lord. In this exercise of faith, he once again was the living example of how to have a heart for God. The richness of this time, even as I am writing, brings the deep desire to have a relationship that is real to my living God.

Many years later, after my dad passed away, Mom lived with my family in Texas, almost two thousand miles away from her homestead. Even at her early to mid-eighties, with one eye blinded and the other only tunnel vision, she took her magnify glass with her giant printed Bible that dad had given her and she read and prayed for at least thirty minutes every day. She became exhausted from the strain of her eyes and lay down for an hour or so to regain her strength. Mom had learned from her childhood, and throughout life, that prayer was indeed an essence of life in the believer.

The Road of Learning

1 Timothy 4:12, 15–16

> Don't let anyone look down on you because you are young, but set an example for the believers in speech, in life, in love, in faith, and in purity.
>
> Be diligent in these matters; give yourself wholly to them, so that everyone may see your progress. Watch your life and doctrine closely. Persevere in them, because if you do, you will save both yourself and your hearers.

The hunger for God's Word was always evident in my dad's life. He would literally study for hours in the early morning or late at night before going to bed. Ever since I was small, his favorite topic to discuss with those who would listen or contribute was Revelations. He loved the book of Daniel because he thrived on seeing consistency in God's truth right from the early ages of mankind. It didn't stop there. He would do research from commentaries and American Britannica Encyclopedias. The latest news in the newspaper and thick informative books sent for as far away as England helped him form his beliefs and thoughts inline with God's Word.

As if that wasn't enough, he would indulge in his self-taught education. He learned from books about gardening. He was an avid gardener and reader in history of all eras, including over forty books just on President Lincoln alone, cultures, biographies, autobiographies, minerals, vitamins, National Geographic books for over fifty to sixty years, and Christian magazines. All in all we counted about two thousand books after his death. Needless to say, if we were on a trip or stopped with a bookstore nearby we knew just where to find Dad. His thirst for what was real and truth he never seemed to quench. It went beyond any degree he could have ever earned.

When I was born, my uncle bought me a New Testament from the Gideon's. I will never forget the day he gave it to me. He gave it to me when I was just beginning to read. The scripture he had written inside it was Proverbs 3:5–6. Little did I know how important those scriptures would be to me later in life. As I sat on my dad's lap many Sunday afternoons, he got me interested in God's dealings as he read about missionaries and their adventures. We had a missionary book club at our church, and he figured he could get me involved in reading as well as be able to have two of us get points for reading it! This surely did the trick. To this day, missionary books are one of my favorite readings. I just love to hear and read how God works in miraculous ways in the lives of missionaries.

Coming home after my first year of college I was thinking I knew quite a lot now. Knowing he was quite a bit older than myself, with so much more knowledge

I inquired, "Dad, when do you get to feel like you've acquired enough?"

He wisely and gently responded, "The older I get, the more I realize I don't know."

That spoke volumes to me.

Mom's studying was of the same depth but by different means. She really got into her oil paintings. When I was a child of four and five, she would take me to her landscaping lessons. Being that I was the youngest and the others were in school, I was privileged to frolic around the outdoors, playing with my dolls and having picnics with my mom. Once again, as I smell the oil paints, to this day it brings back the warm and joyful times I had as a child.

God's goodness was instilled in my mind, body, and soul as a young girl.

I felt like a tender flower growing and basking in God's sunlight, sensing Him kissing me gently with His Love.

The Road of Harmony

Ephesians 5:19(b)-20

> Sing and make music in your heart to the Lord, always giving thanks to God the Father for everything, in the name of our Lord Jesus Christ.

My two sisters, my brother, and I all took piano lessons for many years. My two older sisters took the most years, and I took the least. They went on to play the accordion and organ. I took many years of professional voice lessons even after I was married. My brother and I are still in our church choirs and even cut a Christmas CD. We always had a piano, and it was played, if not daily, bi-weekly, along with my sisters playing the church piano for the morning and evening services on Wednesday and Sunday.

In the later days, my dad and mom's children and grandchildren would gather around the piano when we visited the family, back home in Connecticut. My brother accompanied the pianist on his guitar. We had such fun singing with the instruments for many hours. Even though Mom and Dad didn't have formal lessons, they would enjoy playing and plucking out cords on the piano of their favorite hymns. My mom would sometimes comment, "I do this for my entertainment and for other people's misery." She actually was pretty good. She could play for twenty minutes or so and not even get tired, even when she was in her late seventies.

Not only was there much musical harmony, but the harmony deep within was there too. I remember very few times where disagreements came into any loud discussions. There were many squabbles among the siblings but none that my parents did not know how to subside.

There were many times Dad's kindness and wisdom went hand in hand. For instance, once when I was about eight, we were all going on a family trip to Colorado for a couple of weeks. We piled into our blue and white Oldsmobile, and each of us had our own spot. Being I was the smallest and youngest, my spot was on top of a suitcase with a pillow to sit right behind the driver's seat. These were the days before seatbelts. An incident occurred about thirty minutes prior when we stopped to eat lunch. After we had eaten, we all went to the restroom. I had a small change purse that had all my monies I had saved for the trip, long before we began our journey. I needed one of my older sisters to guard it while I used the bathroom. So, believing my sister could hear me, I had nothing to worry about. I forgot all about it until many miles down the road. When I asked my sister about my purse, she looked sheepishly at me not knowing what to say. She left it back at the restroom. I was absolutely devastated! *How could she have done this to me?* I thought. This was all my life's savings! After making my point that it was clearly her fault, it also was quite clear there was no way we were going back to get it. My emotions got the best of me, and I silently began to let my tears roll down my cheeks. I did not want anyone to know how deeply my distressed spirit hurt. My dear dad looked in the review mirror as he thought wisely and sensitively he requested kindly and assertively, "Okay, everyone, we're a family here, and since Tina has lost her money we are all going to go around starting with me to put some money in this squeeze change purse of mine for her."

My ten-year-old brother was second in line, and he did not see any need in giving any money at all! His thoughts were, *Since it was her fault in not taking care of the purse why should I have to give any of my money for her mistake?* Dad kindly said, "But son, if this happened to you, wouldn't you like it if we did this for you?"

He ended up giving his whole quarter! And around the squeeze change purse went, everyone giving something, and by the time I got it, it was full of money! The harmony was indeed not heard this time with music but with the soul.

The Road of Warmth

Psalm 133:1

How good and pleasant it is when brothers live together in unity?

In winter's cold, sometimes blizzards were a part of my growing up in New England. There was many a time we would go sledding down the hills of the back roads, both in the daytime and at night in the moon light. It was always such fun to ice skate, especially across the street on our relative's pond with bonfires a blazing.

Then there were times of building snow forts. We spent hours and hours cutting icy snow blocks so we could have the thickness and height just right. They had to be able to withstand some long-term snowball fights with our neighbor friends in our front yard.

What a blast that was! Other days we would build our snowmen, at least two or three of them, during the wintertime to be fully dressed with pebbles for their eyes, carrot for their noses, hat and scarf, along with the sticks in the middle ball for their arms. It is no wonder that when we came into the house we were totally worn out from all that hard work and exercise!

I remember one winter so vividly as if it were yesterday. One snowy day it was twenty degrees or lower, and my brother and I had been outside nearly all day, it seemed. At dusk we decided to go in, after making our fort and fighting with snowfalls. We stayed until the four-foot fort started to fall down. We were greeted with a blast of warm air from our home, after coming from the ultra cold air of winter days. It felt so good. We could not wait to take off the outer coverings and frozen mittens. We laid them on the old time radiators to dry out and become stiff as a board. The smell of the clothes drying out somehow seemed even cozier. The Christmas tree was lit. Mom was laying on the sofa watching television, Dad in his recliner chair, reading. After having some hot chocolate there was nothing else to do but curl up with a blanket and fall fast asleep. There was nothing like it. This particular day stays with me, perhaps because of the drastic contrast of the bitter coldness outside with the warmth of both the physically and deep calm psychological affect. The inner growth need of a child was met in the balance of love, warmth, and security. Little did I realize that later in life I would be relying on that warmth to get me through some very difficult times.

The Road of Nature

Colossians 1:10(a)

Live a life worthy of the Lord bearing fruit in every good work growing in the knowledge of God.

It is no wonder why I love nature so much. My mom and dad had green thumbs when it came to plants or gardening for fruit and vegetables. You name it. We ate it. Tomatoes, butternut squash, yellow squash, zucchini squash, yams, potatoes, rhubarb, pears of different sorts, apples, cherries, corn, cabbage, lettuce, grapes, cucumbers, peaches, blackberries, raspberries, peas, just to name a few. Blueberry picking was a non-ending adventure. Ever since I was small, my older sister, Mildred, and I would go to our uncle's place down the road from our home. She would grab a large bucket for herself, take a small rope, tie a bucket around my waste, and we would go to his place. There we picked blueberries to our heart's delight! When we got older, our dad got his own blueberry bushes that looked more like trees. So even their grandchildren could eat some of his most delicious and scrumptious, fresh fruits and vegetables of all sorts. His blueberries were a sight to see. He grew the biggest, sweetest blueberries you could ever see or eat. Many of them were from a nickel to a quarter sized! We would freeze them, bake blueberry muffins, blueberry pancakes, or just plop them by the handful in the mouth. His studying of what makes the best soil, cultivation, and good seeds were the reasons for his great success. Every year we always had a garden, thus we always had plenty of fresh vegetables and fruits to eat, sell, or give away.

Dad and Mom both were good with plants. There were times when other people would want to throw away a tree or flowering plant. They would give it to my mom and dad, and before you knew it, it was growing healthy and tall. They both loved nature.

After I went to college Mom started up a walking group in the town. Some lady friends felt sorry for Mom because she did not have any more children at home, so they suggested going for walks. Well, the rest is history, and to this day, thirty-eight years later, it is still going strong! They take three to seven-mile walks in different places all year long, once a week.

Of course Dad knew his trees like no one else since he cut them all the time in his sawmill. Once when we were on our family vacation in late summer, we went into a trail area, and dad took out his pocket jackknife and sliced some sap off a certain kind of tree so we could all taste it and chew it like gum. There's nothing like the taste of sap off a tree to get your taste buds and senses woken up!

Whenever we would go into a building with wood, he would tell us the kind of wood it was. One of my treasured pieces of furniture is his cedar chest he made for his brother's wedding. He made this beautiful cedar chest when he was seventeen years old. I just love it, as it has the smell of cedar to this day, some seventy-six years later! He even thought of having handles on the side of it for easy carrying.

One of my dad's favorite stories was about when I was about five years old and he asked all of my siblings at the supper table one night, "Who would like to plant some 1,000 seedling evergreen trees with me?" No one said anything, and all I could think about was, *Man, I could be with my dad one on one.* So, I said, "I will!" Dad recalled after planting all of the plants I replied, "Is that all?"

I remember to this day how much I loved spending time with my dad and nature. I was in heaven.

The Road of Honor

Proverbs 22:1

A GOOD NAME IS MORE DESIRABLE THAN GREAT RICHES;
TO BE ESTEEMED IS BETTER THAN SILVER OR GOLD.

One of my dad's favorite Bible verses was Proverbs 22:1. He truly lived up to this scripture as his good name and influence went beyond our home. The house building and sawmill kept him in touch with the town's people. Over the years he had proved himself an intelligent and honest businessman. His ethics were trustworthy, and people appreciated him for his integrity. At church he was the treasurer for over fifty years. He always took the offering, counted it, and deposited it late Sunday evening in the nearby bank that the church used.

Both my mom and dad were very involved with the town's politics. They went to the monthly town meetings as much as possible and spoke their mind when they thought it necessary. Mom would work at the voting polls for many years. One of the neighbors saw the great influence my dad had on their town and kindly said at my dad's memorial service that he was going to miss him in "Wendellville." The influence he had on both young and old was quite gratifying. About a year after he died the town got together and decided to rename the road after him. He and my mom had been living on this road for the last thirty some years. Their children and grandchildren were delighted that others honored him by giving it his name. It is now called Wendell Comrie Road.

What a true man of God he was. He showed the pureness of God's goodness to all around. He wisely showed the fruit of the spirit to others with such humbleness. For he truly lived and showed his life with "Love, joy, peace, patience, kindness, goodness, faithfulness, gentleness, and self-control" as it says in Galatians 5:22, and he did it with grace and wisdom. My dad, most genuinely and sincerely, had the understanding of how to apply the fruit of the spirit in his everyday life to all mankind.

As there are seasons—spring, summer, fall, and winter—of the year, so we have seasons of living our lives. In the spring time of life there is a process of maturation. It's the foundation of development. One begins to learn, trust, and find obedience, discipline, and dependence. This was true in my early stages of life. The formative beginnings began in Connecticut with a family of God's love. Love for God, family, country, and community. It all started in the first light of love.

In the summer time of life it is a transition. It is the time to take personal responsibility, spiritual discipline, hunger for His word, and looking for ones place in working for His kingdom. These are the times when thoughts need to be captive, wanting to be fruitful with the intense need to abide in the Word. This is true of my life as I was entering a new phase of independence—going off to college.

The Road of Purpose

Romans 8:28

And we know that in all things God works for the good of those who love him, who have been called according to his purpose.

Going to college one hundred miles away from home to find my place in life all seemed justifiable. My two older sisters had gone to this very college several years prior to mine. My parents met each other here some thirty-five years before. My brother was a junior at another university. It was my turn. The first several months seemed unbelievable. This country pumpkin had real choices to make, hard decisions of what to become, and a real time to get serious with my walk with God. It was not until my junior year, after many attempts to decide if other occupations should match, that I found myself contemplating becoming a school teacher. An elementary school teacher seemed like the path I was to go. Since both my two sisters were teachers, I didn't think this was my calling too! However, I was wrong about that. Now, my two older sisters have retired, and I am still teaching. All together our years add over a century of teaching. Boy, the stories we could tell!

During my freshman year, I was sincerely seeking His purpose for my life. I sought out godly advice, read about many occupations, took many courses unlike my abilities, and prayed for hours at a time. It was in January in my freshman room that God became real to me. It was an electrifying experience that evening. I became acutely aware of His presence in my life, and He gave me a deeper and newer set of purpose. Even though I didn't have a clear path of my vocation that I was to be in, it was crystal clear that my relationship with God was now real.

My thirst and hunger for God's Word was never ending. I couldn't get enough of His word. Soon my desire to seek Him in a deeper, richer, wider way became more and more evident. I had heard of a church in Boston that was that kind of church. It was evangelical, yet fundamentally rich in teaching His word and creative ways of outreaching to its community. This was just what I wanted. I stayed at Park Street Church for over four years.

In that time it seemed to me I grew spiritually sixteen years. The excitement, the newness, the openness, the desire was just as intense in me as it was in others my age at this church. We were known as "The Seekers." We had weekly Bible studies at someone's house, weekly accountable Bible groups on Sundays from the Seekers meetings. During the summer we would have outreaches from playing sand volleyball along Charles River as others were jogging along the sidewalk and asking them to join us. Later that evening we would have an evangelical get together at a nearby Christian high school. Along with that, every summer we'd get away for a weekend and do a deep study of one of the books of the Bible. English classes were given, using the Bible to teach English every Friday evening to literally nations all around the world. This is not to mention the outreach they would have to the widows, shut-ins, music ministry, or yearly thrust of international and interdenominational missions. Each year they would raise millions of dollars for missions way back in the early to mid seventies. All of this from a congregation of about two thousand! They had missionaries from Wycliffe, New Testament Bible, Christian Jews, Airplane missionaries to name just a few, who were using their rich life experiences in their work for God. I couldn't wait for the next one to speak. I would go to the subway every day for twenty to thirty minutes just to hear the next story. One year about fifteen of us went cross-country in cars to go to Wheaton College to get credit hours on World Missions and Cross Culture Communications. Someone from Fuller Seminary came to teach us. Dr. Ted Ward was another professor who taught us, who at that time had just won the gold medal of the Third World Communications. What a rich and invigorating experience that was.

During my last summer at Park Street, I got to meet Corrie Tin Boom face to face. Her movie *The Hiding Place* had just been released. She was coming to Gordon Seminary for some award and was asked to speak at Park Street Church the same time. When she came up to speak at the pulpit, the place became electrified. Everyone rose up to their feet in respect and gave a standing ovation. We were all mesmerized by her stories of the concentration camp in World War II. She spoke of her Lord so personal and glorious. She told a penetrating story of the demeaning and hateful way the Nazi guards had treated those in her camp and most particularly both her sister and herself. After her father and sister died because of the torturous and hard labor, she would, many years later following the release from the concentration camp, be speaking of God's love. After one of her testimonies, one of the Nazi guards that was in her camp came up from the audience to ask for her forgiveness on how he had treated her sister and Corrie. She could not lift a finger to shake his hand. She was stone silent. Then she asked God for His strength. She knew she did not have it in her to forgive. She slowly moved her hand and she felt such warmth; she knew it came from above. When her hand met his hand, she knew it was God's love pouring through her to forgive this hateful act. What an example of forgiveness that was. Little did I know, her story would be for me to remember as an example through my days ahead.

This was my first experience of meeting some young adults who desired a deep hunger for truth. The excitement in their spiritual growth was intertwined with high intelligence. It was the beginning of my true transition from youth to young adulthood—from the foundation of learning, trusting, obeying disciplining to taking more responsibility in my own spiritual life.

Now that I had my degree in elementary education I was ready to settle down with a life of my own, both career wise and finding that life long mate. I had dated some from the Christian college I went to as well as some at Park Street Church fellowship. However, there seemed to me to be an ever-present reasoning that I was to gleam the characteristics of what a good leader was in the work for the Lord. Not here, but 2,000 miles away someone needed this deep understanding of my walk with the Lord, and his name was James C. Brady.

The Road of Understanding

Mark 12:33

> To love him with all your heart, with all your understanding, and with all your strength, and to love your neighbor as yourself is more important than all burnt offerings and sacrifices.

My older sister had moved to Texas, and she thought I could get a teaching job down in Texas easier than up north. She also had in mind for me to meet someone in her husband's dad's church. My sister's father–in-law was filling in for this church as they were in between having pastors. They had introduced James to the Lord and were mentoring him about God and His ways, reading the Bible with him, talking through theology, and providing good home-cooked meals every time they had a chance to do so.

When he was just a small child, he had two older brothers and a younger sister. They were really quite close in age, all within four years apart. Actually, his younger sister and he were born in the same year! He had a mother and a father and a nanny to take care of them. They had a grandfather and a grandmother on his dad's side that lived quite close by. James would proudly speak many times remembering when his father and grandfather played golf with General Patton in the Korean War. They were both very good at playing golf. The grandfather won many silver-plated items for playing so well.

His mom and dad went to many parties. Their social life was very active.

His life for the most part is a mystery to me, for he could not remember much of his upbringing, except he had mentioned several times that he was an alter boy in the Catholic Church. Later, when we were married, he sought out many hours and years of counseling and even with all this professional help, he could only remember a little of his childhood. He spoke of hurt and abandonment one time. Football became his life in high school. He remembered wanting to have his dad to be proud of him, so he did what he could to better himself to make it big in football. He became an All Star in football, tried the javelin, raced in track, and threw the shot putt. He later would win a full scholarship to Oklahoma Baptist University for his football talent. He ended up not going there and got a degree in business at another university.

There were times when he would remember his father's outbursts. His dad was on the quiet side for the most part, but he had become an alcoholic more severely as James had become a teenager. At times his dad would loose control of his temper. His father had one time become in such a stupor that his outburst became violent, and he was attacking James' mom. James tried to step in so his mom would not get hurt, when the father turned on him and, in his alcoholic state, started after him with a butcher knife.

James went to college, got his degree, and started working in Houston. One day a fellow worker invited him to his church. This was the church that my sister's father-in-law was preaching at. After going a couple of Sundays to church, he gave his life over to the Lord. James was very sincere about his walk with God. He even went to ask his dad for forgiveness if he had spoken unkindly to him throughout his life. James had a heart of gold. He loved to help others. It was in his nature to think of others first. He would often do things for the church. It was a small church where he was going, and he wanted to fix up the place in any way he could. This is where I met him when I came down here for a teaching job interview. As a matter of fact, we even went to paint the church's inside walls for one of our first dates. He would sing from his heart every time he sang about God.

In our one week of meeting it became very obvious to us, and everyone else who knew us, that we enjoyed each others company very much. I was off for Easter, and the following week in April I went to look for a job in Texas. Getting to know him was a delight. He had such a good ear for listening. He would be poignantly listening to every word I said, or anyone else for that matter. His exuberance for God and life was appealing!

I flew back to my teaching job in a Christian school in Massachusetts. James said he would be calling me every evening at seven. He had the Watts line, which was free calling. So, every night my heart would be anxiously waiting for his call. Every night at seven we would talk for over one to two hours. This went on until mid July, when I decided to move down to Texas. I lived with my sister and brother-in-law while looking for a teaching position at a public school. Meanwhile, James and I dated over the next several months, and then we decided to make a date to get married. It seemed to him that December 18 would be a good time of that year to get married. Little did I know then, but that very same weekend of different years my two sisters had gotten married. Since we were all teachers, I guess that was not so unusual as it is a great time for a wedding and long vacation time.

We joined First Baptist Church downtown and got married there. My sister's father-in-law married us. It was a beautiful and sunny but cold day in December. We had the ceremony in the chapel since we knew that most of my family would not be able to come. We also had just started going to this church a few months earlier and had not gotten acquainted with many people there yet.

We ended up staying at First Baptist Church for over eleven years. We even had the privilege of seeing his sister and mother come to the Lord as their personal Lord and Savior. His sister became a member of that church and later met her husand.

The Road of Wavering Times Ahead

Isaiah 54:10

"Though the mountains be shaken and the hills be removed, yet my unfailing love for you will not be shaken nor my covenant of peace be removed," says the Lord, who has compassion on you.

We had become outreach leaders in our Sunday school department and enjoyed meeting others of our age. On weekends we would knock on doors of people's homes that had come to Sunday school. We were there to invite them to come again. It was also a time to lead them to a saving knowledge of Jesus Christ if they didn't know him. We would do this for months if not years. We also had joined the choir of First Baptist of about two hundred plus members. This kept us very busy every Wednesday. We would be there practicing and singing on Sundays in the services. At Christmas time we would perform at least nine pageants a year. We both loved learning more of His Word, being in His fellowship. We never seemed to get enough. A

Campus Crusade for Christ missionary had invited James and me into an "Agape" group. We were a part of that for a few years with some special and devoted Christians. They gave us more insight and bonding like never before. We went to marriage seminars the church had with weekends away to grow in our marriage. It seemed like life could not get any better. Our love had deepened for each other and for God. After I had taught for four years, and we had been married three, we decided to start our family.

By now I had begun to see some inconsistencies with his nature, even though we deeply loved each other. For one thing, his pride over money in the bank was very evident. In the very beginning of our marriage, I had accidentally overdrawn by a few dollars. There was nothing subtle about his inward disgrace. He lambasted me and let me know that my horrible behavior was never to happen again. James' sister was living with us, and, when she heard him go off like this, she stepped in to get him in control of himself. Little did I know then, but many years later he told me that soon after that happened to me, he too had overdrawn the bank account. I did not know anything about it because he liked to keep control of the checkbook.

His changing of jobs was another sign of erratic behavior and gave me some deep concern for our well-being. The first year he worked in an insulation business. He always worked hard and diligently. His bosses always saw the potential in him, and he rose to the top very quickly in all of his jobs. It took only a few months of his hard labor before they put him into a supervisor's position. He was the one who set up schedules, duties, equipment for the men to go out and put up insulation in homes and businesses. One day, after about two years, he had a conflict with his boss about the safety of the men he was responsible for. He told his boss that they needed new scaffolds for the job. The ones they were using had become old and wobbly, and James knew they were unsafe. The more he tried to convince his boss to get new ones, the more the boss got upset with him. Finally it came to a standstill. It was either for James to do what his boss wanted, which was to put these men on the old scaffolds or hit the road. So, when I saw him home early in our trailer home that day, I knew something was wrong. As he patted the old sofa, he said, "Honey I have something to tell you. Come over here and sit down."

As he told me the story, it suddenly gave me an uneasy feeling even though I knew he stood for the right thing. I was thinking, *Isn't there a way to fix the problem another way without putting us into a hole? What is James thinking? How long will it be 'till he gets another job?*

A few weeks later James got another insulation job with some bosses he really admired. We bought a small starter home soon after this job began. Right after our buying of the home we were about to have our first blessing. A baby boy named James was born after three years of marriage. Amongst the differences of opinions there was no doubt of God's will in our lives together. This put a great peace in my soul.

This job lasted for about a year. Then he decided one day, he could start his own business in insulation and make it big. It was to be a polyurethane insulation product spraying into the outside walls. This lasted about two years. It was really a popular product at the time, but problems arose in the findings that it sealed everything too tightly, especially because it kept the moisture in, which was not the best thing to happen here in Texas. He then bought a new kind of insulation business.

Within just a few months, James had made his smart business mind pay off. Not only had he bought the business for a good price, but he got this business off the ground quicker than the prior owner who had it for several years. James had a knack for finding the right product for the right time, but he also had a knack for letting the ones who wanted to take advantage of him whittle into his business life. He had a self-destructive kind of behavior.

The Road of Distress

2 Corinthians 4:18

So we fix our eyes not on what is seen, but on what is unseen. For what is seen is temporary, but what is unseen is eternal.

Within a few months of his business, an older man from church somehow had heard about James and was wondering if he could work for him. After seeing that this man seemed to genuinely want to help James' business take off, James considered making him part owner. As time went on, this friend was using the company's time to "counsel" people on the phone about who knows what. By this time I was pregnant with our second blessing, Kristi, our first baby girl.

I had not been teaching since about two months before our first child, so there was no other means of money coming in besides his business. On a weekly basis, I would clean his sister's house for some extra change to save for the children's birthday parties, but other than that we both believed it was best for me to be home with our dear children. There was never any question about that on either side. I truly was blessed to be home with them right from the start. Not to say it was easy financially, but we were at peace with our decision. There never seemed to be enough money for some basic needs, but it always seemed like he had enough for his whims and wishes of business adventures.

Months and years rolled by before one day his friend got into an overseas project named the "Asher Project." It was to help fellow Christians, whom we had never met, drill oil for Israel. The idea was for us to help make it happen and we would get some of the money it would be making besides helping others. The project got more and more publicity every day, until it seemed the entire church of 4,000 plus member were all talking about it in one way or fashion. Many others in the church were also getting involved. Meanwhile, the influence of this older friend had grown so much on James that he himself later told me he knew deep in his heart he should have let him go way before it got too far. James would be coming home with ideas that owls were of Satan. I tried to convince him that owls were made by God, but he grew more and more fearful of them because this friend had him convinced they were evil. That was the first real sign to me that something was "spooky" about his thinking. It became more and more evident that he was more and more irritable over the simplest things in life.

By now our third blessing had arrived, our second baby girl named Stephanie. The tension was getting stronger by the months. Soon James sold his entire business and talked to his mom about putting in about $5,000 of her savings to put into this Asher Project. The total amount into this project that his friend, his mom, and he came up with was about $240,000. He gave this to his friend who gave it to someone up in Michigan, who was suppose to send it overseas to the Asher Project. However, it stopped there, and this "Christian" man in Michigan used it for his hot bill with the IRS! Now James was working night and day to call this man in Michigan to see if he would sell some of his supposedly multi-million dollar paintings his mansion had on his walls! Needless to say, it never got anywhere, and his depression started with some speed. He did not seriously look for a job, because he felt the time spent in getting his money back was more worthwhile. By now we had grown some deep relationships with our peers at our church and neighbors. The dear, dear friends and my family were speechless and praying diligently.

The tension was so great between us at times we could not have a five-minute conversation without an outburst. I knew I had to do something in order for me not to have a nervous breakdown. The only thing that made sense to me was to take the kids and myself to my parents in Connecticut until he could figure out what he was going to do. The youngest at this time was a year old, and the oldest, going on five.

I needed to get away and breathe. I could not make wise choices under this much stress and pressure. Here we were with no money coming in, three young children, a greatly depressed husband that was undiagnosed as a bipolar, who was unbeknownst to me. Somehow, for the next few months, James got paid from a few companies that owed him back pay. After about two months of his ups and downs, I moved with the children to Connecticut. Our intention was for James to sell the house and move up to Connecticut and get another job. Hopefully life would be better up there.

The Road of Inapproachability

Jeremiah 29:11

For I know the plans I have for you, declares the Lord, "plans to prosper you and not to harm you, plans to give you hope and a future. Then you will call upon me and come and pray to me, and I will listen to you. You will seek me and find me when you seek me with all your heart. I will be found by you," declares the Lord, "and will bring you back from captivity. I will gather you from all the nations and places where I have banished you," declares the Lord, "and will bring you back to the place from which I carried you into exile."

Six weeks later James moved to Connecticut, bringing along a trailer carrying all our belongings. We hadn't sold the house, but we rented it out. James got a job working with my dad, restoring an old 1800s up and down sawmill. It was one of the town's oldest historical buildings. My dad bid his price in restoring it, and the town respected him enough to give him the job.

James loved my dad, and he was glad to be working with him. The haunting of his past mistakes, with the fallen monies never to be seen again, ate at him greatly. His pride had been hurt; the unfamiliar land, living with his in-laws, and so desiring to be back to Houston was making his life seem to lack purpose. He and my mother did not get along at all. Between the inflexible ways of my mother and the wavering ways of James our relationship was unapproachable. Any unkind behavior from my mother, whether purposeful of not, made James' harshness come out even more.

Eventually my brother, just two doors down from parents, recognized the difficulty and opened his doors even though he had not been married long to his new wife. I'll never forget the picture of James carrying down our chest of drawers on his shoulder to prove we weren't going to stay another minute with my mom.

At this time I was home-schooling my oldest because he was five years old, and I did not want him to get behind, nor did I want him to go to school up there if we were to go south sometime soon. So, I took all I had been teaching first graders and started teaching him every day. Kristi, our middle child, now three, wanted to be a part of this action, so I made up some simple ABC coloring for her to do. Stephanie, the youngest, was just starting to walk. We would have schooling at my parent's house and live down at my brother's house.

While we were there, we went to a Baptist church about five miles from the house. We really enjoyed the fellowship, the services, and soon got involved with Approved Workman Are Not Ashamed- A.W.A.N.A.S. Club. We had never heard of it before. Most of the south had not either. The children all enjoyed it so much. It gave them something to look forward to and they were able to meet some children their own age.

Fall came with its beautiful colors and crisp air. I was so glad my whole family got to feel autumn the way I remembered it. Soon came winter with its arctic winds and playful white snow. The kids even got to build a snowman with their daddy. This was his first time to experience such distinct seasons as well. January came around, and the 1800 up and down sawmill project was finished. Massachusetts Institute of Technology University somehow had heard about it and came down to inspect it. They said in all their years they had never seen a better-constructed project.

James became restless and stated that he had to go back to Houston because he had to finish meeting some bills, and he thought he could get a job down in Houston. Well, I was not ready. To me it felt like I was going back to hell. I could not see what he hoped to see going back to Houston. But I knew if I did not go with him then I probably would not ever go back. So, off we went to Houston in the mid winter to find yet another job.

The Road of Diligence

2 Corinthians 4:8, 16–17

We are hard pressed on every side, but not crushed; perplexed, but not in despair;

Therefore we do not lose heart. Though outwardly we are wasting away, yet inwardly we are being renewed day by day. For our light and momentary troubles are achieving for us an eternal glory that far outweighs them all.

When we were going home we stopped in the Carolinas for the night, with the trailer behind our Oldsmobile. James thought it best to park it directly across our room so we could watch it from the window. The next morning our trailer was gone. Everything we owned except what we had in our suitcases, gone. Even our wedding pictures were gone. Later the police found it, after we had gotten into Texas, and told us that the burglars had dragged it into the woods and burned it all. I'll never forget James' reaction after he saw our missing trailer. He had all of us get down on our knees beside the bed and pray for the ones who stole our trailer. I felt my husband was starting to be the leader again in our home. That gave me such reassurance that we were indeed doing the right thing.

As we were approaching Houston, my heart sank in deep despair. The uncertainty of jobs brought memories of insecurity of our finances. Once more, we had rented our home out so where would that leave us to live? We did know for a few weeks we were going to live with a friend and his family who graciously took us in, but we also knew it was not going to be for long. It turned out that we lived with them for about a month while James was looking for a job and I was continuing my home schooling. We got an apartment on the other side of the city from our home, and James had got a recruiting job for an aviation school. This was commission based, so this meant I needed to bring in some kind of supplementary money.

Every Sunday we went back to First Baptist, and by now the church had been hit hard with people using their tithe for the "Christian investment." Brother John, the pastor, once telecasted his sermon of how this investment had "sheered his sheep." It had devastated many families financially. We went back to the Sunday school class of our age group. After the devastation of the loss of all our belongings we had no furniture, and we didn't have insurance on the contents. Somehow the people at church heard about it and they began to gather the items from pots and pans, silverware, furniture, and bed sheets to help us in our need. The Sunday school teacher felt led to give us $1,000. We were so thankful for the outpouring of God's people helping us in time of need. Our brother-in-law asked us if we wanted to buy his mother's car for a real special deal. It had not been used that much and was in great condition. Now I could have a car to go to work. A dear friend of ours said her husband threw papers in the morning and made $600 a month, so I thought I would give it a try. I felt it was a good supplement, and yet I could still be at home with the children. I ended up working there for about five months, getting up at 3:00 a.m., rolling the heavy city papers until about 4:30 a.m., loading the car, and delivering them by throwing them over the car and into the darkness, trying to land them in the correct yard the best I could. After a few months they had me do work inside the office instead of throwing them. I was glad to do that instead. Meanwhile, I began substituting at the nearby neighborhood schools on the days James did not have work. When I was not teaching, I was homeschooling. The kids' education never lost a beat. They kept up the pace that I wanted their schooling to go.

I remembered how God was watching over us in another matter. Stephanie, our youngest, had now learned to walk and was walking around the apartment we were living in for a few months. One warm spring-like day, we opened the window on the second floor. She heard her brother and sister outside playing right below us. I was sitting down on the sofa next to the window when suddenly the screen gave way as she was pushing against it. I grabbed her and fell back with my heart racing and thanking God for saving my baby. I called the manager that day and had them screw in the screens and told them they should have done this for every window in the complex.

The Road Back to Work

Psalms 107:28

> Then they cried out to the Lord in their trouble, and he brought them out of their distress.

Summer came, and we had told the people who were in our home that we had wanted to live there after June. We had been gone from our home for over a year. We were so thankful that we did not lose the house and had someone renting from us all that time. We finally got back to our 1,400 square-foot home, and it felt like a mansion. I felt so blessed to call it home. My emotions were ready to get back and start all over again.

We stayed at First Baptist for another year. It had left a very important mark in our hearts. For after all, this is where we had gotten married and grew into God's fullness. We met our dear married friends, we made early in our marriage. Many a year we were in the pageants there, had all our babies dedicated under Brother John, and many other dear memories. This is also where our oldest, now in first grade, had gotten his first grade Bible from Brother John. This was something that First Baptist did for all the children who had finished first grade.

Since we were almost thirty minutes away from First Baptist, and by now we had three growing children in different activities, it seemed wise for us to look for a church nearby so that our children could get more involved in a church closer to our home. So off we went looking for a church to take the place of such a mega church as First Baptist and fill in all the holes of needs as First Baptist did.

One thing we were looking for was an opened minded church to consider AWANAS. We knew it was not readily heard of down in the south, not even First Baptist, but we just loved it so much. I even looked it up to see where other churches had it, when we first came down in January. We went miles away to a church that had AWANAS on one of the weeknights, because we knew it was such a wonderful ministry.

It was not long after this that we found Calvary Baptist Church which was right down the street, about two miles. It was a much smaller church of about two hundred plus members. It had all we were looking for—sound doctrine, a good choir, and an open-minded pastor who, when asked if he would consider AWANAS after telling him what it was, said, "You know, I'll have to pray about it because I don't want to get to heaven and hear God saying, 'Why didn't you open those doors? I could have had many more children come to know me.'"

James was asked soon after to be the commander of AWANAS. So for six years he became the commander. I was the leader for cubbies, ages three through five, and guide leader up to second grade. Every week during the school year, we would go and have a great time with the children, learning scripture upon scripture, hiding God's word into their hearts. There were so many generous helpers giving their time to further the kingdom each and every week. Many years later, after we left, people told us, "It's still going strong. It's got a different thrust than when James led it. It's never been the same since he led it!"

We would have a yearly Pancake Breakfast served by the leaders on a Saturday morning in February, just to get the parents more involved and let them see a little of what AWANAS was all about. Then once a month we would have a missions thrust to give updates by missionaries or stories of what was going on in the world for Jesus. Every week the children would have sing-a-longs with a video of Christian songs. These were just a few things we would do to make AWANAS a part of each of our lives.

James found a job at an insurance company soon after we moved back to our home and became a salesman for the insurance. It didn't take him long before he was one of the very top salesmen of 6,000 employers. His debit area was in the third ward downtown. The people just loved him. They always trusted him and grew to respect him as their friend. He worked that field for many years. All of his work was by commission, so he worked as smart and diligently as he possible could. We had become more financially stable as his finances were quite steady but that did not mean we had enough to save any money. Our bills were being paid for, and at that time we did not have any credit card usage to speak of.

I was busy keeping house, tending to the children's needs, smocking dresses for our girls, and cooking home made meals. There never seemed that we had enough money to buy clothes, so I figured it was more economical and creative to make our girls' clothes. It got to the point that sometimes it was a loosing battle to convince James we needed items for the household, like a lamp or paint to personalize the children's rooms. Yet the very next day, we had a discussion; I noticed he bought himself a watch or something he wanted. When I mentioned the item he bought and that he had argued for several hours the day before about buying a needed lamp, he lost all reasoning skills and became like a victim of a caught crime. He blew up saying he would return the item. I was trying for him to see the inconsistencies. He would not hear of it. This made me feel guilty. Had I done something wrong? My abilities were being tested. How unfair I was to not see his needs!

After about a year of getting back to our home, we decided I would need a part-time job. I started to work for a private pre-school as a certified teacher for four half days a week, just a couple of miles down the street. This was just right. Our son was going to full-time school by now, our middle daughter was going with me for free to the pre-school, and the youngest stayed with my sweet sister-in-law just down the way from our home.

Things were somewhat stable but still no means of putting away money for the future. After about a year, James became more and more aware of the financial needs and was then putting some pressure on me to go back to work full time. Our son James was then going into the second grade, Kristi in kindergarten, and Stephanie was old enough to go to pre-school with me. School had started up and we were in mid-September when he insisted I go full time to work, so I looked around for a job. But the only one I could find was in a large city school. Needless to say, that lasted for only a couple of months, and I took my job back at the pre-school.

This meant I could be with Stephanie full time for one more year. This was a blessing to me as I felt it my duty to stay with my children as long as I could at their young and tender age. That next year I got a teaching job just about a half-mile down the street from the pre-school, which meant I could come by for Stephanie's pre-school parties, birthday celebration, and in sickness I could pick her up really easily. I still felt like I was being her mom the closest way that I could and work. The older children would come by after school to my place where I was teaching. That way, I was there to oversee their homework, given them snacks, and talk with them about their day at school before we went home. This went on for over five years.

The Road that Marked Beginnings of Unraveling

Proverbs 25:28

Like a city whose walls are broken down is a man who lack self-control.

James so loved his children. He really wanted the best for them. He had become a coach for several years in baseball at the YMCA for our son James. He was the best coach in many ways. One year there was an unruly-mouthed child on the team that was used to getting his way, yet he was an excellent baseball player, especially in making home runs. Then there was another child on the team. He was sweet as sweet can be but he had two "left feet" and was so uncoordinated. I do not remember if he ever did hit that ball. One evening in the game we really needed the homerun, but James had just reminded the unruly boy that if he did not start controlling his mouth he was not going to play at all. Well, it happened. James sat him out for the entire evening. His grandmother came out of the bleaches and thanked James for going through with it because that was exactly what he needed! James used the two left feet boy up to bat. He always had them take turns no matter how good or how bad they played. That season we came in first place! He always wanted to help the "underdog."

During those formative years for our children, James was not only working full time, coaching on the side, serving as commander in AWANAS, but he also was going to school for his masters in hospital administration in the Houston area with a full load of 18 hours.

By this time I was working full time for over five years, and we were looking at moving up north about thirty miles. We finally moved into a subdivision, northwest of Houston. We had gotten our children enrolled into the district and started to go to Champion Forest Church. This is where I met some moms that were praying for their children and the schools they were attending. The groups name is Moms-In-Touch. James was doing well enough that I did not need to work, which lasted about three years. So I was privileged to pray every week during the school years for their adjustment, friends, teachers, studies, etc. for three different schools.

James' behavior started to get further away from the center of our belief system. Even though he read the Bible nearly every day, went to church every Sunday, had weekly Bible studies, tithed, and even memorized God's word; his spirit was becoming further and further away from the man I married.

During these three years, we met some fine Christian people who became our closest friends named Chuck and Barbara Lloyd. They are still to this day the closest friends anyone would ever want. Not only did I have my Moms-In Touch groups, but these people are fine missionaries who have been with the Navigators at that time for over twenty-five years. These people are dedicated to the ministry of discipleship. They would go to the ends of the earth if someone needed them to. Their hearts could be defined as humble, servant like characters. We learned to trust people who could handle our deepest secrets. They point to God for all the answers in life and really connect, whether it is in small or big ways, with human beings and their needs. There is no doubt God had us hook up with these fine people for many, many reasons.

James' behavior started to unravel as a yarn from its ball. He started accusing me of being righteous. He became more critical of even the coffee drink that I would make him. He was hyper-condemning of the children and being more aggressive with their discipline. One day our thirteen-year-old son wanted to redecorate the bedroom he was in to better fit his taste instead of the baby walls that were there before we bought the house. After we all agreed it needed something done, we went to look for some new wallpaper. We picked out two kinds of wallpaper, a border wallpaper, paste, spatula, bucket, and some wood for the chair rail he wanted, along with varnish, at a discount place. My son and I were trying to hang the top half of the wallpaper as straight as we could. In walked James, angry for some unknown reason, about the straightness of the wallpaper. He then went up to the strips that took us half a day to do and tore it off the wall saying something like, "If you can't hang it straight then don't hang it at all." Then he stormed out the bedroom. We were devastated. We did not say a word for a few minutes. I just started to pray out loud for the situation and for the Lord to give us peace.

Another incident was when our middle daughter, Kristi, was insistent on making a point, and James was totally annoyed to the extent he wanted her to sleep out in the garage for the evening. James made it known that I was not to go out there to her. I was frightened of him but worried about Kristi. How was she to sleep out there? I do not think I got any sleep that night, but the next day Kristi told us she looked around the garage for boxes to make a little fort and used her blanket to soften the cement floor.

My mind was racing as to what to do. Should I cry, yell, be obedient to the husband that was abusive, pray? Where had the kindhearted man I had married gone to? Days went on with our ups and downs, but I did not know where the issue of all this anger was coming from. I remember praying one day, and I felt God's presence to come downstairs and read some books on my shelf. Searching for the right answer, my eyes caught the Bill Gotherd series on character building. We had gone to several of his seminars in the past; our dear pastor at Calvary wrote some of the protection series in it. I felt God wanted me to look at honesty. As I read it, I suddenly prayed for James and his honesty. I prayed for him to be honest with God and with me. That evening I told him what had transpired during the day. He sat there and listened and said, "I really wanted to tell you something, but I didn't know how, and now that you said this I'll tell you."

It was to tell me that he had been doing things that he was ashamed of, things that were not of God and wanted forgiveness for. His promiscuous behavior had led him to deep sin. I was devastated. How could he have done this?

Throughout our almost thirty years of marriage we went to what seemed like hundreds of hours of counseling. It was not until later that James was diagnosed with bipolar by a psychiatrist. Some of our Christian counselors were free services and some were not. There were some non-Christian counselors paid through by our insurance. Some were coming out of our pockets that were extremely expensive. There was really only one kind of counseling that really affected him in a meaningful and productive way and that was the Christian Twelve Steps to Freedom. But this was years later, so the counseling we had prior to that only aired out what we already knew—a troubled soul that could not get peace with his past nor present.

Not long after the talk of his waywardness, he had an automobile accident where someone hit him from the back while he was on the job. He saw doctors, physical therapists, and finally even had back surgery. This took about three months or more before he was out of pain. Later he got a settlement from the whole incident and it paid our house off.

James' father died about this time, and he went down to Brownsville to go to his father's funeral. The family was all there, but, by the time he had gotten back home, James did not want to speak to any of his family. He had become angry, but I never actually remember what had transpired, except it had something to do with all of them helping his mother out financially, and James had not planned on that one.

A few months passed, and, one Sunday while going to church, we started talking to some people of our age, and they found out that James had eleven years in sales of a well-known life insurance. They were looking for individuals who had a college degree, experience in insurance, and a sharp, warm personality to open up a new insurance agency for a very reputable, well-known insurance company up north that wanted to come south. Houston area was one of the major cities they wanted to start up. James fit the mold. He was soon to open up his very own agency from scratch with the help of references from the new insurance company.

The Road to Something New

Ephesians 5:13–16

But everything exposed by the light becomes visible, for it is light that makes everything visible. This is why it is said: "Wake up, O sleeper, rise from the dead, and Christ will shine on you." Be very careful, then, how you live--not as unwise but as wise, making the most of every opportunity, because the days are evil.

Starting a new business like that meant we would need to move over to the zip code of where the new agency was to be. We looked and looked for homes until finally we decided to build our own home in that zip code. I was thinking about the three kids needing to move schools and churches and an unstable dad that blew up over small, seemingly insignificant things. So, why not build a home to get them into seeing the process and slowly but gradually move over to Spring with hopefully some excitement of adventure. It seemed so logical to me yet I did not say a word as to my real reasons why I wanted to build a home. All in all it took around a year to complete from picking the land to moving in.

It was not quite finished when school started for the kids, so, since I was not working, I took them every morning and picked them up in the afternoon for about two months while going nearly thirteen miles one way. Sometimes I took two trips because the high school and the middle school's time to start and finish were so different.

Bipolar is such an incredibly debilitating illness. Sometimes I wonder if it is an illness or a disease. A disease that eats away a personality and livelihood, as cancer only this sickness you really cannot see because it is all in the mind. All one can see on the outside is self-destruction. Self-destruction of their hopes, dreams, desires, ambitions, talents, and gifts. Sometimes this illness takes a very short time to see what destruction has taken place and for others it takes a long time to see the ramifications. For my husband, it was the latter. There are what is called rapid cycling and slow cycling. In all my reading on it there are people who can self-destruct quickly, by throwing items around the room, breaking things, and overdosing on pills all within a few minutes. Then with others the process is much slower and harder for a person looking on to detect a problem, especially if one is not educated to know such things exists. This was me. I had not even heard of bipolar until almost four years after moving into our new place.

Everything seemed to be new at first. We had a new job for James, a brand new built home, new neighborhood, new schools, even a new church. The adjustment took much effort but this took some of the time away from the tensions at home. James was starting at the bottom line of opening his new business, picking out the colors, blinds, etc. of his new place. The insurance company had set up desks, cabinets, secretaries, and even names for potential clients in his zip code area. The company wanted the agents to get a head start and be very successful so they did everything they could to make it happen. It was now up to the agent. All he had to do was sell his already believable product—insurance for home and car. This was James' expertise—a born salesman. Within just a few months he had it up and going. After the third year he was neck to neck in his competition with other agencies that had a much higher price range of houses, a few miles in both directions of his place. Prices of homes he had were somewhere around $85,000–$150,000, whereas the other agencies homes were anywhere from $200,000–$500,000. So no one could deny his abilities. However, not only was he placing this much energy into this new business, but he once again began to draw individuals into his life that would later radically self-destruct.

The main individual was one who lived in the area of business and wanted to buy some insurance; we will call him Dr. Dot. He was much older and spoke about his adventurous life quite freely. He showed his supposedly many credentials, from being a physics professor at a prestigious university to an entrepreneur of many sorts. Dr. Dot had interests that led this elderly man to commodities of oil, gold, and silver. This is where James and he got hooked up in interest. Soon James was spending even more hours at work than ever before, learning these ideas, finances of it, connections, bonds, etc.

I became more and more leery and even had nightmares of it all and started praying diligently on my knees. I felt very vulnerable and insecure about it all, yet I wanted to encourage James to be his best in whatever he did. Did this mean something even bigger than the insurance business that was given to us on a silver platter? Was there any security in this? Was there any truth to all this?

The Road of Troubled Waters

Luke 8:23–24

> As they sailed, he fell asleep. A squall came down on the lake, so that the boat was being swamped, and they were in great danger. The disciples went and woke him saying, "Master, master we're going to drown!" He got up and rebuked the wind and the raging waters; the storm subsided, and all was calm.

I had taken a teaching job after my first year in our new home. Things were tight because we were starting up a new business and building a new house. So, I went back to teaching after being out for three years. I really never thought I would be back, but things had changed. That particular year was extremely hard for me. Not only had I been out for three years but reentered into a new world of teaching to the test, a new environment, etc. I also was dealing with difficult behavioral children and an undiagnosed bipolar teacher on my grade level. She was acting more like a lead teacher than the lead teacher herself. She enjoyed telling others what to do and how to do it. Others followed with no questions. They actually seemingly enjoyed her authoritative spirit. I, for one, did not think much of her tactics but did my best to keep the "team spirit." About three years later she too was diagnosed with being bipolar.

During this time things started to happen at the house. We all started to feel like we were stepping on eggs shells around an explosive, volatile expressive husband and father. I started a journal. It was part of a prayer journal and part reflective journal of the day's events. There were many an afternoon, evening, or weekend I would go into my closet, not wanting anyone to know how distressed I was, especially my children. It felt at times there were sixty to eighty-foot walls of waves about ready to crash and gulp me up in a terrible storm from all directions. It was much like what I think the fearful disciples must have felt when Jesus fell asleep in the terrible storm all around them. I would cry, read the Bible, and write in my journal, waiting for God to reveal to me how I was to handle the issues of the day while I was in the closet. Somehow I had convinced myself what James was accusing me was true. Although he did not actually say it, I made inferences to say to myself that I was *not* good with finances, *not* good at being a cook, *not* good being a wife, nor a mother nor teacher. Then *what* was I good at anyhow? I had lost all my confidence in who I was as a person.

Just at those deep times of despair, one of my sisters, Janice, would call and give me a Bible verse God had revealed to her for me. Here she was in Ohio, and I in Texas, and she did not know the everyday grueling situations I was going through, yet the scriptures just pierced at me, for the relevancy of the scripture was so precise. Scriptures such as Psalms 18:1–3 "I love you. O Lord, my strength. The Lord is my rock, my fortress, and my deliver; my God is my rock, in whom I take refuge. He is my shield, and the horn of my salvation, my stronghold. I call to the Lord, who is worthy of praise, and I am saved from my enemies." Or Matthew 11:28 "Come to me, all you who are weary and burdened, and I will give you rest. Take my yoke upon you and learn from me, for I am gentle and humble in heart, and you will find rest for your souls. For my yoke is easy and my burden is light."

The children and I were seeking counseling at our church at this time. I went for over a year. My concern led me to write to Dr. James Dobson, a renowned Christian counselor in Colorado Springs, president and founder of Focus on the Family, about needing prayer for the distress I was in. I wrote to Joyce Myers after reading her book, *Beauty for Ashes*, and I even wrote to the Promise Keepers—a Christian men's group that I trusted. All of them got a lengthy six to eight hand-written notebook paper letter that was written at different times but revealed the tumultuous times that my children and I were experiencing on a daily basis and seemed to be getting worse. My hope was that these experienced Christians would give me strength and hope through wisdom and prayer. Only heaven knows just how many prayers had gone up for my entire family.

I dared not read the journal for over a year, until one day I felt I could handle the turbulence that would be reveled. After about the second page I could not bear it any longer. My question to myself was- how did I get through that *one* day? All the emotions were at the surface, and I shut the book with the affirmation that this was not my problem; it was his. Right then I prayed, "Lord, he's all yours. Do with him as you will."

That afternoon James had come home. He looked at my face and replied pointing his finger at me, "You've given me over to God, haven't you?"

In which I replied, "I sure have."

He retorted back, "Good, now I can do what I need to do."

I had no earthly idea what he meant by that nor did I have a clue of how he knew I gave him over to God, except my tension on my face must have been gone.

Every day seemed like an entire lifetime; emotionally, physically, spiritually, and mentally, I was strained to my limits. Isaiah 26:3 says, "You will keep him in perfect peace, whose mind is stayed on You." I had a steady focus to do just that. My prayers were of constant vigilance for His protection on us as a family. James' obedience to Him, as well as praying daily Stormie Omartain's book on *The Power of a Praying Wife.*

Even though things were array, James wanted to help missionaries. There were times when we would earnestly talk about the way we could disperse the money from the investments to many God fearing Evangelicals so that others could know Him as their personal Lord and Savior.

James had decided by now that he should go to Indonesia with Dr. Dot to determine their possibilities of buying commodities of oil, silver, and gold. Dr.

Dot had told James of some bonds he had and knew of others that could be worth in the millions. So James perused his entrepreneurship and went overseas for a week. He came back with a new insight from that trip, after seeing the gold mines and high officials in Indonesia. He wanted things to end with Dr.Dot. His mistrust in him was very evident now. He wanted none of his secretaries to answer any of Dr. Dot's calls or to have any business related to him. It was a 180-degree turn around. When I asked him why he felt this way he said, "All the so-called 'good connections' weren't anything but possibilities." One night he said that Dr. Dot's eyes told him everything from lies, deceit, and deadness to his soul. He said he knew if he had any more to do with Dr. Dot this would be his life too.

Tragically it was too late for James. His boss had already warned him a few months prior to stay away from Dr. Dot. But because his will was stronger than his desire to do what was right, his boss told he would have to go. There were other things that compiled to his boss' decisions but this was the main reason. James never got bitter or angry, for he knew he had not heeded good advice, and now it would cost his livelihood, his goals, his stability of finances, and his dignity. Would it cost him his family too?

He came home after this with all his family pictures, awards, and paperwork in a box. He told me what had happened, and I remembered the feelings were similar to our first year of marriage when he came home to tell me he had lost his job. This time though, it had more ramifications to it because we had one senior in high school, one sophomore, and one in middle school.

The Road of Anxious Moments

Matthew 6:34

> Therefore do not worry about tomorrow, for tomorrow will worry about itself.
>
> Each day has enough trouble of its own.

It says in God's Word that is so comforting in Isaiah 43:1(b)-3(a) "Fear not, for I have redeemed you; I have summoned you by name; you are mine. When you pass through the waters, I will be with you; and when you pass through the rivers, they will not sweep over you. When you walk through the fire, you will not be burned; the flames will not set you ablaze. For I am the Lord, your God, the Holy One of Israel, your Savior…"

This was a time of holding on to my faith in Him. It was time to "be still and know that I am God." In Psalm 46:10 and Psalm 46:1 "God is our refuge and strength, an ever-present help I trouble." One of my favorites since childhood is found in Psalm 121:1–2. "I lift up my eyes to the hills—where does my help come from? My help comes from the Lord, the maker of heaven and earth." After a few weeks went by James started to become anxious and began to question his abilities. He began to question his abilities in judgment of people. He began feeling hopeless, guilty of not keeping his "silver plated job," worthless, helpless, and he began losing sleep. He read his Bible, and devoured the book *Search for Significance*, written by McGee. He talked about his past with a keen desire to understand his thought process and why he had ended up giving this perfect job away. Within a few weeks he was really losing contact with reality; he was in a psychosis state. He was not getting much sleep, if any, and pacing back and forth in the night in our bedroom.

One night he remarked, "Oh, oh, Christina, just wait till you get to heaven; you will have such an awesome position. You are the bride of Christ."

To this I replied, "James, the Word is speaking of the body of the Church not one person."

To that he said, "No, it's you who are the bride of Christ. This is your reward for all the difficulties I have put you through."

Somehow I had convinced him, the next day, to see what the church could do to help us. We wanted Christian counseling, so we thought it would be a good idea to start with our church. This went beyond their expertise, so they led us to a Christian psychologist in the area. When we got to the new office, we sat down and talked for over an hour or so, and he determined we needed long-term care and persuaded us to get into our insurance system to see a psychiatrist. It usually takes several weeks to get in to see a psychiatrist, but since this counselor called that very afternoon we were at the psychiatrists' office. He had been a psychiatrist for over twenty years, and he began asking James a series of what seemed like twenty or so questions. After answering "yes" to all of them, the doctor looked up and said, "Well this is easy, you are a classic bipolar."

I must have stared straight through the doctor's eyes for at least a minute thinking to myself, *You mean there's a name to this hell we've been going through?* Somehow, I was a bit relieved to have a label to this way of life. Soon I was asking him all kinds of questions and then he told me to read a few books and proceeded to give me the names of them. As I wrote them down he told me this would help me to better understand this disorder.

He prescribed some medicine and then James became frantic about the time of the day. It was past the hour that most pharmacies would be open. We had to ask the doctor for the twenty-four hour drug stores and call them to make sure they would be open before James felt secure enough to leave this office. He prescribed medicines for depression, manic, sleeplessness, and he was on two other prescription medicines from our family doctor for high blood pressure and prediabetics. He began his meds that evening. The next few days, I went out and got all the books the psychiatrist had recommended and read them from cover to cover just mesmerized at the stories of this disorder. Meanwhile, James was getting more sleep, but he was also getting weaker it seemed in his countenance. By now, he was exercising on his bike and was losing twenty to thirty pounds. We even had his pants altered, so he would perk up his feelings of pessimism. I thought he would feel more productive if he could help me grade some of my second grader's papers. He made so many mistakes in grading that I had to give up that idea. His abilities to think, walk, or talk quickly was almost impossible for him. After about a month, he started to wonder if he was ever going to see himself as he was before. So, one morning as I was going to work, he said good-bye as he usually did, to each of the children as they were all heading off to school. Stephanie was the last to say good-bye because her middle school started later than all the rest of us. During the day I always called in the afternoon and talked to him about the day. That afternoon there was no answer. I tried to calm myself down by thinking that he sometimes goes outside to walk around the house. When I got home, the two older children were eating and getting ready to go to Kristi's basketball game. I asked, "Where's dad?" They said, "Oh, he's sleeping in bed."

Well, right there I knew something was drastically wrong. He could barely sleep at night. What was he doing sleeping during the day? I ran into the bedroom to see. He was knocked out, snoring with papers written out to his sister and me, with his insurance papers next to it. Reading only a sentence of his death wish, I ran to call 911. The kids were already in the van, ready for me to take them to the game. I felt split feelings about not letting them know what really happened and telling them I had just called 911. I told them what had happened, and then I called his psychiatrist. He tried to calm me down, so I could go get all his medicine and try to figure out what he had taken an overdose of. I got all the pill bottles and counted one by one to see which pills he had taken. It turned out it was a handful of sleeping pills. By the time I figured it out, the EMS team was there, asking what he had taken. The police came right behind them, asking to see his suicide note. There we were trying to get James up and talking to him, meanwhile the stretchers came and later James was strapped to them. Our dog, Sugar, a miniature Sheltie, just stared at all the commotion as Stephanie walked in the door. Stephanie began crying and blaming herself for not saying anything before. For she believed when her dad said, "good-bye" this morning he meant it in a different way, a way that meant forever. "I just knew it by his eyes," she went on, and repeated this throughout the day and for many days later. I would tell her no one knew, but she insisted, "Yes, mom, I knew."

We went to the nearby hospital to get his stomach pumped, but, because he had taken it so early in the day, they decided to give him charcoal to drink to absorb the toxins. When we came to see him, his mouth was covered with black coloration. Friends and family came, trying to help and console. Once his body was stabilized, after many hours, they sent him to a psychiatric hospital many miles away. We went to see him every day, but he didn't remember any of us. He would talk to us, eat with us, watch television with us, but not remember us after we left. One morning as he was getting ready for the day, he lost his balance because of the medicine and banged his head hard on the side of the nightstand. It drew blood, but from that point on he remembered everything that went on. It was as if he woke up from a zombie state of being.

He must have stayed there for almost two weeks before he came back home. This was when I had to take just one day at a time. I could not look too far ahead, but I had to depend on my heavenly Father to carry me through the days ahead.

Abraham, in Genesis 12:1, tells us that he walked by faith. He did not know the future of what he was to do. Nor did he know where he was to go. He trusted in advance, taking hold of God's perspective. This was where life mattered to him. This was where I, too, lived. This is, as the old term goes, "Where the rubber meets the road." I was taking that walk—step by step—trusting God, living by faith.

The Road of Class A Misdemeanor

Psalm 32:9a

Do not be like the horse or the mule, which have no understanding...

One thing about it, James would always want to read through the Bible of which he did many more times than for me to count. He believed it to be the true and living Word of God. He always gave more than 10 percent to his church and at times more than 15 percent. He taught me things about giving. His giving was not only in money, but in everyday happenings; he had visions for tomorrow, hopes, dreams, and faith to back it up. However, at times his faith was intertwined with overly good, euphoric moods of which I will speak later.

After about three months, he started to go back to feeling like himself again with medicines and seeing his psychiatrist and counselors. He started looking for a job in a sub-standard insurance. This lasted less than a few months, because after he was still being stabilized on his depression medicine, his judgment of anger control was not the best. At this particular place, one took numbers for the potential customers. This way the people working there all got a fair chance to gain customers to sign up with them. His customer had been there the day before and told James he would be back that next day. When he returned the next day, James was at lunch. The man was just leaving as James came back from lunch. Another lady who was working there was dealing with the customer. James tried to explain to her that that particular customer was there the day before, and it was his customer. Well, things were tight in "closing the customer," so the battle was on. The woman was on the phone to call the manager, and James rudely grabbed the phone from her. Another fellow who was working there thought James was attacking her, so he jumped him and the fight began. Swinging, grabbing James' tie till he almost chocked him to death, then the guy went out to get his crow bar from his car. Meanwhile, the woman called the police. In walks the fellow worker with his crow bar and takes a swing at James. James grabbed him by the throat, and he told me later that he knew it was only seconds more and the man would be dead, so in a split second of decision he released his hands and said, "Enough is enough!"

In walked the police and off went James to the downtown jail. Not knowing any of this, I was concerned when supper came…no James. Darkness came…no James. The business had closed by now, and finally, about midnight, I get a call to come downtown and pick him up at the county jail and pay bail. "Do what? Where? Now? Why? What happened?"

I called a dear church couple, and without any hesitation they said, "We'll be right there." Off we went at midnight, downtown, to get him out by now one o'clock in the morning. He had a Class A misdemeanor against his name. I asked one of the clerks that worked there, "What does that mean, Class A misdemeanor?" She said, "Oh, it's nothing really, it's called a simple assault, it's like having a traffic ticket against your name."

Back home we went looking for yet another job. It was about this time when my school district I was working for changed insurance carriers. This meant that we had a new list of psychiatrists to choose from. The new insurance carrier did not cover the psychiatrist we had been going to. This did not set well with James. We went to a new psychiatrist, but the doctor wanted to change the medicines. All James could remember was how horrible he felt when he first got on the other medicines. His "old man" syndrome, his suicidal attempts, his worthlessness, hopelessness, and sleeplessness all made him extremely apprehensive about changing the medicines. Besides that, he had established a friendship, a trust level, with the first psychiatrist. So, for a few times, out of pocket we would pay so we could continue to see his old doctor. But being that there was only one income coming in—and on a teacher's salary at that—with three teenagers, it was not something we could afford! So, the next best thing James decided to do was have our family doctor we had known for years prescribe the old meds from the psychiatrist. This went on for several years.

Things became a little more stable. James decided to go back to his own business once again. This time he decided to start up another business—sub-standard insurance business of his own.

The Road to Owning an Insurance Business—

A Second Time Around

Proverbs 15:22

Plans fail for lack of counsel, but with many advisers they succeed.

He rented a place off one of the main roads in Houston for his business. He rented from this place for a few months, and I noticed his behavior became more and more irritable. He was taking his medicine, but he still was not interested in seeing a new psychiatrist. He was having more and more intrusive behavior with the one he was renting from, until finally he packed up his equipment and rented down the road to a truck sales place. After a few months this did not work out. He rented a space of his own in a nearby strip center, selling his substandard insurance. The children and I all tried to help him from mail-outs to copying insurance claims to setting up computers and even running around to buy food for his big barbeque cook-offs, to bring more people in. But still his restlessness and poor judgments were looming over him.

By now it was our middle daughter's senior year. She was in a talent show at the end of the year that the school was sponsoring. We went as a family to hear Kristi and her boyfriend, later her husband, get up to beautifully sing part of an opera song. After their singing and the clapping, her dad was making loud intrusive comments from the audience and carried on, so it naturally made Kristi very uncomfortable. She let him know just how she felt after the show was over. He came up to say "hi." James, making a poor judgment call, became aggressive and denied that he had done anything wrong. His childlike behavior lasted right through Kristi's time to graduate a few days later. He never showed up, "…to show her a thing or two." That was his comment when I called to remind him to come to the graduation.

Just before her graduation time, a minister came to visit our church. He brought out the point that the toughest battles are *from* God—and sometimes blessings are dressed up as curses. How more relevant could that have been than at this time in our lives? Then he spoke of scriptures from Job about commitment. He asked, "Will a person serve God when life turns tragic?" Job 1:21. "The Lord gave, and the Lord has taken away; may the name of the Lord be praised." The Lord told Job He had a right to do what he did, and the reason is to *trust* Him. There is a meaning to our sufferings a meaning to all that we do.

I was both aggravated and disappointed in James' behavior, and yet I wanted to make the best of Kristi's graduation day, for her sake. We filmed the ceremony, and ate out before and after the ceremony. We all found things were very difficult to get beyond the emotions of it all. Soon after the graduation, Kristi informed us she wanted to join the Air Force.

The Road of Tough Decisions

Psalms 16:1

Keep me safe, O God, for in you I take refuge.

James' mom was diagnosed with bone cancer and only had a matter of months before she died. Many matters had to be discussed with his sister and brothers. By the time her funeral took place, I felt it necessary to go with James to Brownsville for support. I knew they would keep their distance from James because of the unresolved problems from the past. It just seemed the right thing for me to do. I was glad I did.

During that summer we heard about a program that one of the large churches in Houston was sponsoring for Dysfunctional Personalities. James said he wanted to go. So, we drove about forty-five minutes every Sunday afternoon, for about eight to ten weeks. There were only a handful of people there, but James absolutely loved going. He would keep on saying, "If only I had this when we first were married." We would have homework every week. Judy, the woman who put this together, was a Christian licensed counselor.

One afternoon she assigned us homework to write down the very first memory we could remember and label its time frame and emotion. That night when we got home, he got a legal-sized paper and, in his smallest handwriting, went on and on for hours and hours. By the time he finished, it was about ten legal-sized papers long, front and back, in the tiniest writing you could imagine. I thought it valuable for him to share with me only if he wanted to. He shared just a couple of things, one of which was the feeling of abandonment when he was a child, seeing his parents from a window to leave for another party and being left with a nanny.

I could not believe what I was seeing or hearing. Was this the same guy that said he could not remember anything of his childhood? It was very therapeutic to him, and he felt he was getting somewhere when he did the exercise for homework.

Right before this exercise, she pointed right to us and said, "You are the only couple in here, so I'm going to warn you. Be careful. Be very careful this week because whatever you do, those feelings are going to be right on his shoulders." Little did I know what a week it would be.

Not more than a few days later, my dad passed away from a heart attack, up in Connecticut. At this time Kristi was finishing up her boot camp in San Antonio. The graduation ceremony for the Air Force was going to be on Friday during the day, and the flight out of Houston was on Friday evening. I tried to talk James into flying out of San Antonio so we could have more time with Kristi, but he said it would cost too much.

We went to San Antonio Thursday evening and stayed over night. We really enjoyed being with our daughter. The next morning we went to the Air Force graduation, with the beautiful and magnificent precision formation of the air show along with the strategic formation of the marching flights. After this we were to eat a small bite somewhere on the grounds and leave to go home to Houston for the flight to Connecticut. James began to enjoy his stay with Kristi and thought his time with her was beginning to "heal" from past problems as he was talking to her in line for the food. What we did not foresee was the amount of people who were at this same fast food place on the grounds. It literally took thirty to forty minutes just to place our order, and I knew it would take more than four hours to get to the airport because of Friday's traffic in Houston. So, I thought it wise to try to convince James to leave before we ate. After about three minutes of trying to convince him, he suddenly became irate! He was going to fix that problem and so into the car and did we speed! We went over ninety to one hundred miles an hour all the way to Houston! He said, "Shut-up and don't say a word!" Off we went road raging and drag racing. All the time I was praying, "God keep us safe. Place your hand over the car."

We came to Houston in record time—one and a half hours. After he got there, he pulled out my luggage from the back of the van and threw them on the ground and said, "Have a good trip!" He tore out of the airport drop off place as if he was an irresponsible teenager. I was devastated! I called the kids from my cell phone to warn them of their dad's temper and to be careful. Then I called James' sister and asked her to keep an eye out for the kids while I was gone to my dad's funeral services. I called the airlines to see if I might get my money back since he was not going. I was so relieved when they said we could, for we really did not have that $500 for him to go anyway. My sister was going on the same plane for the trip to Connecticut. I was so glad she was going, for I needed some release from what just transpired. She was shocked as she listened to the furry over what? As I was up there in Connecticut, my mind was so taken away by all the drama; I just thought that it deadened my emotions of my dad's loss. I could not think straight with what was I supposed to do. Should I go back to that angry, bitter, explosive man? What purpose would it serve if I did? Could I possibly take a split from work? What about our youngest, still at home in her senior year? As time went on, I found myself asking these kinds of questions to my relatives. I felt like I was taking up their time to console me instead of them consoling my mom or my brother and sisters for our dear dad's loss. But the intense problem needed some solution and quickly.

The Crossroads for Change

1 Peter 5:6–7

> Humble yourselves, therefore, under God's mighty hand, that he may lift you up in due time. Cast all your anxiety on him because he cares for you.

The fact that my mom had only one eye to work with, and that eye was not very good because she had tunnel vision in it—it kept her quite needful of someone helping her even though she tried to be independent. The loss of a partner of sixty years was one adjustment all by itself but with all the other factors of getting around, cooking, etc, was something all of my sisters and brother had to come to grips with. My solution was to move up to Connecticut, help her to get things simpler, substitute in the schools, and bring Stephanie up to finish her senior year in Connecticut. The only problem was how was I going to get her? Since I had a plane ticket I thought it would be wise to come down to Houston, get the van that was in my name, convince Stephanie, talk to counselors, pack, and go without

James knowing. It worked. While James was at work, we loaded the van up to the max. We had just a few hours before he would come home. My biggest concern I had for Stephanie was for her not to see her dad commit suicide in front of her and she blame herself for it. Even though I did not tell her my true feelings, I felt it best for her wellbeing to come with me even though I knew it would be extremely hard as it was in the beginning of her senior year.

Off we went after staying at a friend's house the night before. It took a couple of days to get to our destination, but, after the day on the road, I called James to tell him what we were doing. He knew after seeing my clothes were gone. Stephanie had left him such a sweet note, leaving her teddy bear for him. He tried to talk me out of it, and yet he realized how badly he had treated me under such stressful circumstances when my dad died.

My mind was made up. I called the school to tell them I would not be coming back so I could take care of my mom. I used all my sick leave before I resigned. Soon after returning to Connecticut, we started to clean the house my dad built and where my mom was living. We cleaned from attic to the basement, sixty years of my mom and dad's marriage's accumulation. It was some ordeal!

Mom still had a bit of independence about her, enough to tell us what could and could not be thrown away with everything she could lay her hands on. This took an incredible act of patience on our part. My brother was up there, after his work on the weekends, cleaning the basement with assistance from paid help—his son and Stephanie.

For a few weeks I was with her the whole day until I got the paperwork done to substitute teach in the town. I would leave her the phone number of whichever school I was substituting for that day. Then I would come home to cook for supper. I tried to keep her routine like she had it before Dad died as much as possible. On Thursdays I took her to the fish market, and Fridays we went shopping for groceries. Sunday we went to church. This was Stephanie's and my new life's happenings. We were cleaning the house nonstop for months. We were trying to put the house in shape so we could sell or rent it. We knew that mom could not live there much longer, but where would we place her? She was too mobile for a convalescent home and too dependent for senior housing, so I looked into a full-time caregiver at the house and assistant living. We looked at the kind of service, recommendations, the cost, the whereabouts, etc. I knew in my heart there was a "behind the scene" as to why I was up there. To tell you the truth, I would not have thought about it twice if this had not happened with James and me. I never would have come back to Connecticut and taken care of my mom. After all, I had a job and a child in her senior year. And my brother was up there to take care of her…but I did not realize the enormous responsibility it took to make all the decisions that needed to take place. My brother could not have handled them all by himself. He had enough to do getting the finances in order, cleaning up the landscape, painting, cleaning the basement of the house, etc. He did not need the load her emotional needs, care, and whereabouts of her future. Was this God's way of waking me up to help my mom and brother? We all took a part in handling our elderly mom and in deciding what was best for her.

As days went on James would call several times a week. I listened at first just to make sure he got going in life without depending on me. We talked about his job, his walk with the Lord, his tomorrows, his counseling with Judy. But this time he was paying eighty-five dollars an hour to see her. We talked about my job and what I was planning to do.

One day around Christmas, I decided to go see him for Christmas and our anniversary. I also had been seeing a professional Christian family counselor in town who was highly recommended and my mom's pastor who had his masters in counseling as well. No one was suggesting I divorce him, but they were giving me suggestions as to how to handle the situations. Mom's pastor had worked for Salvation Army on the side and had many dealings with bipolar victims, alcoholics, and drug abusers. He said they all really had a lot in common. Stability was always a problem and that was why it was so important to have some accountability along with correct medicines and a good, understanding, and qualified counselor for his condition.

It was decided, after seeing him at Christmas, that I would come back to my very school I left and begin in February. Up north it is very hard to get a teaching job, even if one had been on the substitute list for many years. My money was wearing down, and I wanted some stable money coming in. We had set up mom to see an overseer for the next few months and possibly after that to go to an assistant living place down in Mystic. This place was renovated from an old school house, the one my dad had been to when he was a child. It was in beautiful condition after it had just been decorated with its setting over the Mystic River. She was not really ready for such a place. She did not feel comfortable like she had at her home. So, we thought maybe the best way to figure out what to do was to have an overseer be at her home most of the day.

The Road of Last Chance

Isaiah 41:10

So do not fear, for I am with you; do not be dismayed, for I am your God. I will strengthen you and help you; I will uphold you with my righteous right hand.

My school in Houston that I left had a place for me. I would even be able to get my full year in because I used my sick leave, which lasted until December. Working from February on till the end of school would be enough days to call it a full year. What a blessing that was, as money was getting very scarce. When I left in February, Stephanie was still going to school, finishing her senior year out at the school I graduated from many years before.

After I left not more than a couple weeks went by when my mom bumped into a doorway, fell back, and ended up in the hospital. She stayed there for a couple of weeks then entered a convalescent home. She ended up doing this twice. She was at the convalescent home when I went up there in early June to see her. My sister Mildred, from Houston, came up and convinced her to come down south to live with her two daughters. So, in August she did just that. My sister took care of her for a couple of months after this my mom moved in with James, Stephanie, and me. She lived with us for the next three and a half years until she died.

Mildred's husband died soon after my mom came to live with us. He had suffered with juvenile diabetes for many years and died of a heart attack. Soon after Mildred sold her home and lived with all of us. In our 3,000-plus-square-foot home, we all had our space to live.

The next three years was full of decisions, jobs, talks, and angry outbursts from James. At this time he went through at least four different jobs, selling cars and trucks. His mood swings did subside somewhat after the first year or so with my mom there. But he did have some mean outbursts in the beginning of her stay with us. One such response was with my mom getting on the phone to tell her friends they needed to pray for James. Everyone was at work except James. Mom did not have good hearing and did not realize James could hear what she was saying all the way upstairs. In his foul mood, he came downstairs and yanked the phone out of the wall and threw the phone outside. My dear mom had taken her purse and cane and walked outside our house to find a neighbor. We only have nine homes back where we live. She ended up at our neighbor that has a pet dog named Peaches. Mom knew her from our wheelchair walks we would take about three times a week. Peaches was almost like her body guard. They had a real sweet connection. Mom knew where Peaches lived, and I think subconsciously she knew it would be all right if she came to Peaches' home for help. My neighbor called my school where I was working. I came home as soon as I could. Stephanie had come home for her community college, and we decided together to call the police from our neighbor's house. They booked him for some past warrant for his arrest of a "hot $5,000 check." The police thought that he would be in the jail for a few months, but instead he was just in there overnight. The judge threw his warrant out because it had happened some five years before, and the check was not made out by him but by another person.

There he was back at the house before I could think of what I should do next. I did think of buying another house and letting him sell this one. The more I thought of what to do the more he prayed and thought of what was going on with himself. He slept upstairs going over the book *Search for Significance* by Robert McGee. He read this book and the Bible seeking help again.

One night I had a real interesting dream I believe came from the Lord. I was dreaming that I was by myself walking out in a dark field with mostly prairie-looking tall grass. I stopped at this dead-looking Oak tree. Suddenly I heard this growling sound only to find a snarled angry dog ready to take a bite out of me. I thought of climbing the old Oak tree, but then I felt myself lifting up, up, up and gently gliding up in the air, floating through the air as if I were an angel. I soon realized if that dog had not been there, I would have taken my next step into a dark pit that was about forty feet deep with a football field circumference. I was floating toward one side of the field, when I saw a ten-foot heavy, iron-gated cave area. One door was a jar. My illumination of my body was lighting the darkness below and showing some dead bodies that were piled on top of one another. They were all male, and only one was still alive but barely. This one was in the center of the opening area of the gate, and the body was faced down. It had some kind of light coming from its head. I suddenly started thinking in my dream, *What if the cops come and see this, and they'll think I killed these men.* So I started to fly over to the backside of this cave area. I gradually landed on the same type of prairie field, yet there, in the middle of nowhere was a trailer restaurant. It was crowded, and the two-inch cut blinds and windows were open to let the late fall evening breeze come in. All of a sudden I heard and saw James pacing up and down the restaurant, going in between people to get from one side of the restaurant to the other. He happened to see one of our pastors and called out to him, "Lucian, have you seen Christina?" He responded, "No James, I haven't seen her."

As he pressed close to the window and rolling his hat in his hand in a nervous sort of way crying, "Christina, just give me one more chance." I knew he could not see me.

Then I woke up. I sat up in bed and contemplated about that dream for days. I really believe those dead bodies were representing something of James' difficulties in his illness or personality that have been overcome by prayers, and the one last light of his well-being was still there to be dealt with. I felt myself becoming tender toward him, but I wanted to see some evidence that he truly wanted to change. So after about three weeks or so, I began to trust him little by little.

He got a job at another car place as a salesman. Meanwhile, our finances were not doing that well from the instability of his job weavings. So, within the next five years, we refinanced our home two times and each time consolidating our bills. The mortgage was about $130,000, and, by the time the five years was up, it was over $183,000. I thought we would never get ahead. On top of that, the last refinance was ARMS, which meant in two years it would go up to the going rate for interest! I was under the impression that it was one that was a fixed rate, which it was for two years. James, however, was in the mindset that his big adventures were about ready to set us free, and therefore it would be paid off in two years.

One of my prayers in the journal I wrote on March 22, 2002, was, "Is this what my marriage is going to be like for the rest of my life? No spiritual leadership, no direction in his life, no romance, no financial stability, no communication with his children so to speak of, no joy, no peace, no fun? "Through sickness and health"—it never even entered my mind of mental illness. Can God get the glory from a life like this? What depth of blindness is this on both our parts? I cannot see answers to these perplexing issues. Where's some balance in all this?"

The Road to the Last Few Years

Colossians 3:1–2

Since, then, you have been raised with Christ, set your hearts on things above, where Christ is seated at the right hand of God. Set your minds on things above, not on earthly things.

During this time of working in car sales, he met someone that had connections to yet another adventure that was mystical to me. This time it grew into the infrastructure of Nigeria, Africa. There was to be a force of Christian aide for medical, schooling, road building, etc. for the sake of doing for others in the perspective of God's work.

The more he talked and spoke about it over the next year and a half, the more it mystified me. As far as I know, he never spent any money in it, but then again I really don't know to this day if he did. The heart of James was always for mission-type work and to be used as God's servant. No matter how realistic or unrealistic his adventures were this was always his main thrust.

It was at this time that James decided, after fifteen years, to go back and pursue his master's degree in hospital administration, since all he lacked was his thesis. He decided this would be good to have since he would be in leadership over some hospitals in Africa. His thesis was in the area of a specific cancer of Africa vs. United States and their diets.

After working about two and a half years at four different car dealerships, he decided to thrust his time and effort into giving pointers in writing a book giving advice to others on how not to fall into the ways of emotional hooks when buying a car. He gave excellent pointers, examples of people's stories, what to say, what to look for, how to get the best percent on your interest, the best price of the car, and many other "insider" understandings when buying a car.

This lasted for over several months and all without going to work. He kept saying, "I'm going to have to get a job soon." He even got on the Internet to look for jobs—gave his resume to many places but never seriously looked for a job. So between doing his research for his masters, calling on Africa adventures, and writing his book, of which never got published because of the cost to publish it, his time was taken up. Little by little, over several months, his thought process got more distorted. After talking to so many people in person, or on the phone mostly, about the Africa adventure, he started to visualize the happenings more seriously. He visualized the money for all this adventure would be coming in soon because of the "leaders" in the pursuit were saying so. But, the monies never came about.

It was around this time my mom went to the hospital and within a few weeks, she died with complications of clotting to the heart. James began thinking because of his book it was going to be a big hit in the book market, and he would need to print over a million copies. He was going to be known for the powers God was going to give him to "move mountains," speak any languages, and heal people over in Africa.

By now I became really concerned for his realistic belief system. I started to ask him about going to see the doctor. His response was with gesture, "You think I'm going off my rocker again, don't you?" I told him there are similar happenings in his behavior as many years ago. But the more I tried to convince him to see someone, the more he became agitated. Soon, we were two months behind our house payment. I had to take out my annuity to cover the back payments.

Right at this time, my sister, who was living with us, got married and moved to California. This was Stephanie's last year to be home for the summer as she was on her way to Dallas to go to a university. We had been thinking about moving to a smaller home since our nest had become empty over the last few months, so we put our house up on the market.

I felt so sorry for the lady that was our realtor. She did not know us, but she could feel tension that was going on in our home at the time. She later told me she is not easily intimated, but she said she was with James. For you see, James had some preconceived idea that another lady was suppose to sell it because her name meant something spiritual to him. His behavior became more and more erratic. Racing thoughts, excessive compulsive disorder, increased energy, restlessness, little sleep, denial of anything wrong, unrealistic of his abilities and powers, until one day he claimed he was the bride of Christ. I gently tried to remind him about the time he had thought that I was the bride of Christ. I was hoping he would see that this meant he needed to see the doctor. Instead, his response was, "Yes, but I got the wrong person."

Well, the time was getting shorter for Stephanie to be at home as it was already in the middle of summer. My mind was working over time now. My biggest priority was cleaning the home up as quickly as possible, so we could sell it. Every night I would think of what to do the next day. For one reason I felt I had to keep him busy, the other was to clean the house from attic to the garage. We cleaned windows, blinds, ceiling fans, attics, closets, and books. We gave away extra clothes, making many trips to Salvation Army and our church. Each day it seemed like James was becoming more and more irritable, until I could hardly tell him anything without him thinking I was not being submissive.

After much talk with a friend, Stephanie and I decided something must be done before he got any worse. There was many a night that I would sleep on my side toward him because I was afraid he might want to suffocate me in the middle of the night because I disputed his thinking that he was "the bride of Christ." I happened to be listening to James on the phone one day. The next thing I knew James was talking to these strangers I had never met from the Africa connections and was telling them my bank account number, how much our house was worth, and other personal financial information.

I began to panic, thinking what am I going to do if he gives all my monies away? What security is that? How do I stop him? What do I do after Stephanie is not here with me? God soon revealed the answer to me in an indirect way. It hit me that when my kindness turned me into being an enabler, it is not good for either one of us. It is not healthy; I must not be that to James.

I wrote in my journal just what I told him. "I told him yesterday (Sunday) that I will no longer have him on my insurance as of the twentieth of August. It is paid up until then." I also wrote, "I expect him to pay his own bills from now on—his credit cards, look for a job by July 5. It needs to be a stable one taking the rough times with it and not quitting. If he needs to switch jobs, make sure it is with no lapse time in between jobs. The other thing I told him is to make sure he sees a doctor, both physical exam and a psychiatrist. What he did not know was that I could not and *would not* do this anymore. There is no more time to do this.

My prayers had been to be debt free, save for the future, not to spend needlessly, nor control money miserly. This is the wholeness that God wants because it is balanced. He needs to be responsible for his actions just as I am for mine. James needed to live in reality just as I needed to have tough love for him. May God get the full glory as we go forth." Then I added, "This illness has divided us. There is no need for forgiveness on either part. We need to live in the *present* not the future."

We had bills, and my hope was to get out of debt and for him to get a job. I wrote a quote in my journal from a thought I once heard, "It's like hoping for rain in the drought of twenty-eight years." There had been so many "deals" that never came through. I continued, "I love the man who is energetic, extremely talented, warm and loving, yet the other man takes over and is self-centered, egotistical, self-destructive, lives in the future, is not realistic, and shoots the one I love in the foot."

After the house was cleaned, I decided to move in with a friend; Stephanie went with me until she went back to school. I needed some space to think, and think quickly. I was on "survival instinct"—that's what I called it. I believe others call it the "flight mode." However, I could not see any other way than to divorce him. I needed to break the ties before I had no finances at all. There is no such thing as legal separation in the state of Texas, and I did not want my money to be spent to whatever he was wanting to do with it. I gave the analogy of it as if we were out on a boat in deep, deep-sea water, and James threw out the anchor. He grabbed it and clung to it for dear life. I was on the rope that was pulling the anchor down right behind him, and I was frantically trying to cut the rope for survival.

The Road to a Refuge

Nahum 1:7

The Lord is good, a refuge in times of trouble.

As soon as I moved out, I ran to the bank to change my account. I found a lawyer and went to work to divorce him. Days went by without him knowing where I was. He knew I was seeking out for a divorce because of the papers that were drawn, but other than that I only communicated by e-mail. I gave him names of doctors to see at a prestigious medical school here in Houston.

In the middle of all this, I began reading Lon Solomon's book on *Brokenness*. He wrote about God's focus, which is on the *depth* and *quality* of character that those in Christian leadership must have if the power of God is to be revealed. "For every great task God has always prepared a man or woman first. In God's service, brokenness always precedes true usefulness. Broken Christians are people who are willing to get real and honest with God and with themselves. In Christian brokenness Christ's followers are approachable, teachable, sensitive, turfless, and forgiving. By approachable he meant no vain ego to defend.

Teachable—is willing to listen to others. Sensitiveness senses other people spiritually, emotionally, and psychologically. Turfless means that one has no personal turf to protect. The Lord alone defends me. Forgiving can see mistreatment, and when we forgive it actually enables God to work in their life. People will feel relaxed, comfortable, and unthreatened around those who have been broken by God. God uses it to make us a channel for the Holy Spirit's power. Brokenness and greatness for God always have and always will go hand in hand. If we will walk with God with unquestioning trust, God will bring us through triumphantly. He has never and can never fail those who trust him without hesitation."

That seemed like Lon Solomon hit the nail on the head, as I knew this was a part of God's refining me.

An e-mail he sent me was on August 23. It said:

> Christina, I want to take this time to thank you for the many years of prayer and suffering you have done for me. I pray and know you will see the results of your efforts and prayers for me to the glory of God. May God grace you with His mercy and a fulfilled life in Him. Love, James

He got a job at Wal-Mart during the days and a security type of job at night. By September he was saying that when he went to the doctor, two nurses had told him he was *not* a bipolar, and the doctors did not know how to help his sleepless nights. Who knows what he told the nurses and doctors.

By October he had lost over thirty pounds; by the time three months had gone by. Some of it was because of fasting for over thirty days, some because of exercising, and some because he was on a cleansing colon binge. October 2, he wrote, "I know you only want the best for me. I can only hope God directs me in a way that honors Him. May God grant the two of us mercy. I love you, James."

Later he wrote how his gifts and talents were in the way. He kept on being insistent that the monies would be coming from the African dealings. He wanted to pay off all the bills and would give me more than enough to live on for the rest of my life, even if I was not married to him anymore. October 9, he wrote to the people that dealt with the African adventure, "...should anything happen—pay Christina the full amount... and should death befall me..."

This made me fully alert of his depression. I finally talked with him, but because he really knew how to cover up things, he made it sound like this was what needed to be done because it was supposedly so much money to come about.

A few days later, I got a phone call from my neighbor. She said she saw an ambulance come to the house. I was across town and asked her if she would go over to the house and see if she sees anything. She did, and she peeked into the kitchen door window and saw blood on the floor. I said I would be right over there. I was with Barbara and Chuck, my friends that I was staying with, and they decided it would be better if they went over with me to the house. We cleaned the blood all up as it was in between the chair backs, on the phone, on the floor, and on the welcome rug. I called the nearest hospital, where I thought he would be, but they said he was there early in the evening but was not there anymore. We called the police, and they came soon after. We started to fill out a missing person report, when we decided to call the hospital again. This time they gave us more information than the first time we called and said he was there but was transported down the road to the psychiatric hospital. The police gave his code number, and we must have waited twenty minutes or so to find out that he was indeed at this hospital. When we found out he was there, the police did not need to continue the missing person report, so he left.

My friends and I went down to the hospital where James was, at about 9:00 p.m. Even though it was after visiting hours, the workers there let us in to see him because they knew he did not have anyone to be with him. When we saw him, he looked like a lost puppy. He was cognitive that we were there and made conversation but did not contribute much unless we asked him direct questions. We talked to the nurse for some time, and she was so positive about James' doctor because he had good success with bipolar patients. He had been working with them for over twenty years.

When my friend and I went to visit him over the next few days, we could tell his thinking skills were not that sharp. Although he did keep mentioning the fact that he could not believe he had cut himself several times on his wrist. He became more nervous when we talked about day-to-day happenings. One time we were with him as he was eating supper, and he said that he did not want to go back to the house. Even though we were separated, he could go back to a very nice place. We were trying to sell it but had not got any serious bites on it as of yet. There was a couple from

California, who saw it on the Web site, that seemed interested but nothing confirmed.

He said the doctor was extending the stay as long as he could with the insurance. Later the doctor told me that he asked James if he could stay beyond the time, but James stated over and over again that he could not do that to me. The bill would have fallen on me, and he knew that I just did not have the money to extend the stay. So, after several days at the ward, he was sent home. I was working when they let him go home, so Chuck went over there to pick him up. He said it took both nurses to direct and stand him up to go to the car. Chuck said James could not remember how to get home. "Was the house south from here (the hospital)?" he asked Chuck. Chuck told him, "No, it's northeast." Chuck knew this was not a good sign because James had such a great sense of direction.

He got home, and I came over after work. It was around suppertime, so I told him I was taking him out to Denny's. He reluctantly came with me with a smile. We both ate a salad as we talked. The doctor had put him on Lithium and other medications to get it into his system as fast as possible and to be stabilized and as quickly as possible. The doctor intended to change it after a few weeks to some new medicine for his illness.

I took him home and mentioned I would be back the next evening at about five to scrub the toilets for the couple from California that was coming to see the place in two days. I told him God loved him very much, and I loved him as a sister in Christ. My emotions had changed into an agape love for him. He said, "Christina, no one, no one in this world would have ever showed me more love than you. You have always been there, stuck with me, and cared for me. I know you care."

He opened the car door as we were now in the driveway and said, "Thank you for the meal."

He shut the door, and I watched him go into the lighted house and turn out the light in the living room as he went back to his bedroom. That was the last time I saw him alive.

The Road of Trusting Him

Proverbs 3:5–6

> Trust in the Lord with all your heart and lean not unto your own understanding; in your ways acknowledge him, and he will make your paths straight.

The next day, I came back over about 5:00 p.m. to clean the bathrooms; I knocked at the door, opened it, and called out his name. I thought it was a bit strange, but he liked to take walks, so I put my mind at ease thinking he went out for a bit. As I was gathering my items to wash the bathrooms I noticed the dried washrag had been hanging there for more than a day to dry over the shower door. That was strange as I knew he always took showers every morning. I started to call out his name again, walking upstairs and suddenly I thought, *Don't be surprised what you see in the garage.* I went out to the garage, and there I found him with the motor still running, gagging fumes, and his dead body at the wheel. Immediately I opened the garage door. My millimeter second response as I looked into his face was - *He's at peace. He's whole. There is no more war going on in his mind!* He looked so peaceful. It just stood to remind me of how much restraint he must have used as he was here on this earth. His thoughts, he would tell me especially in his manic time, were racing so much he would often tell me, "Oh, Christina, if you only knew what else is going on in my mind. There is so much I'm not even telling you."

I would respond, "James, you've told me enough." He did not have the racing thoughts and need to restrain his marathon mind. There was no more tension—he was at peace.

I ran back to the house and called 911. Then I called my son on my cell phone. I said, "James your dad ended his life, I need you here. I don't think I can do this alone."

He came right over with my daughter-in-law. Within what seemed to be just a few minutes the police came along with the ambulance, neighbors, friends, and our pastor.

I was standing on the edge of the patio, and I could see all of this going on from a panorama view, even James' body in the car. Suddenly, as if God was speaking to me directly, He said, "Trust in the Lord with all your heart and lean NOT unto your own understanding but in ALL your ways acknowledge me…and I'll show you…I'll show you your paths." It was spoken with that emphasis just like that. In all the commotion of the day, the Lord stilled my thoughts to remind me that He is in control. It took me a minute or so, but I then realized that this was the very same verse James and I had taken for our almost thirty years of marriage.

James called Stephanie at school in Dallas. She came right home. Kristi and her husband were called. They got here as soon as they could from North Dakota. My sister Mildred was in California. She was out here the very next day. My sister Janice's son, flew in from Washington D.C. Funeral arrangements were being made with my church. Family, friends, neighbors, my coworkers, and church people were all being so supportive and helpful. They all seemed like angels coming in and out of the house, flying in and out to support the family any way they could.

Once all the family had come in to town, we stayed at my son's house. So we all slept on beds and blow-up beds for the next few days. This seemed so comforting to be together and talk, cry, laugh, or hug at any time of the day. It seemed so right to be at their house at this time of our lives.

Everything happened so quickly as calls were being made to find burial plots, asking friends and relatives to speak at the memorial, creating a PowerPoint, and on top of that I had to inform the realtor of what had just transpired. Then, looking at his life insurance that he had for over fifteen years, I then realized it had lapsed just three months prior. He had that particular life insurance for over fifteen years, of which would have paid off our house. We made decisions upon decisions and more decisions. His body had to be autopsied because of the way he died, so we decided to have a closed casket and have a small gathering around his gravesite the evening before his memorial service.

The next day we had the memorial service at our church. We played his favorite CD's of praise music in the background while a beautiful sequential pictures of his life were being shown. This lasted about ten to fifteen minutes. The eulogies were given from his sister to preachers, missionaries, neighbors, and friends in chronological order of how his life unfolded. People have told me, "I've never been at a memorial service before that spoke about that person and really knew him like they did with James," or "That memorial service truly gave honor to his life with such respect," or "I've been to a lot of memorial services before but none like this one. He touched so many people. He really had a great influence on people."

After the ones who spoke, there were written comments from friends and relatives of their eulogies that the pastors read. The last one that was read was my tribute, and after I explained Proverbs 3:5–6 and how the Lord stilled my thoughts to remember that He is in control. I wrote, "The happy times along with the tough times of our marriage are something I'll never regret, because it has made me to be the person I am right now. I first saw his heart for God, and this is what attracted me so deeply to him. James had a heart that deeply loved the Lord. He wanted to serve him with everything he had and more. His talents and gifts were many, and as much as his illness let him, he was giving all that he had. He loved his family—his sisters and brothers, his wife, children, and their mates he adored. He only wanted the very best for them right from the start.

One of his very favorite songs was one that was written a long time ago, back in the late 1960s by Kurt Kaiser. Kristi and her husband sang it so meaningfully.

"Pass It On"

It only takes a spark to get a fire going,
And soon all those around can warm up in its glowing;
That's how it is with God's Love,
Once you've experienced it,
You spread the love to everyone
You want to pass it on.
Chorus: I'll shout it from the mountain top
I want the world to know
The Lord of love has come to me
I want to pass it on.
What a wondrous time is spring,
When all the trees are budding
The birds begin to sing, the flowers start their blooming;
That's how it is with God's love,
Once you've experienced it.
You want to sing, it's fresh like spring,
You want to pass it on.
I wish for you my friend
This happiness that I've found;
You can depend on God
It matters not where you're bound,
I'll shout it from the mountain top
I want the world to know
The Lord of love has come to me
I want to pass it on.

When the chorus of the song came to the line, "I'll shout it from the mountain tops," Kristi started to break down, and her dear husband was right there carrying on the message and giving her strength to carry on throughout the song. What a sweet, sweet touch to end the memorial.

The Road of the Days to Follow

Jeremiah 29:11

For I know the plans I have for you, declares the Lord, plans to prosper you and not to harm you, plans to give you hope and a future.

The very next day after he past away, James got a letter from my insurance company. It addressed the fact that he stayed at the facility of the psychiatric hospital one day too many. It stated that since he did not speak of hurting himself, he would have to pay back that one day. Well, this led me to talk to a lawyer and his doctor to look into the matter more closely. The lawyer believed that insurances truly abuse the psychiatric patients more than any other area of illnesses.

The doctor told me that when he started out many years ago, he would keep his patients for twenty or more days, where his colleagues kept their patients fifteen or less. I asked what the outcome was of the extra days that he kept his patients there. He revealed to me that his patients were not seen over and over again like his colleagues. It just takes a long time before the levels of the brain can be stabilized. The doctor also told me that, a few years prior, the board of insurance went all the way up to the Supreme Court to fight about the psychiatric doctors keeping their patients too long in the facility. They complained that the patients were kept too long and it cost the insurance too much money. Then the insurance company lost their subscriber after the first year because the cooperation that bought from these insurances would choose another insurance company. Therefore, they never got to see that patient get well nor the money returns.

If James had stayed at the facility any longer, he would have had to tell everyone at that place that he intended to hurt himself. Otherwise the insurance investigation would be able to find someone who did not hear him say that. James' doctor also told me that James was very leery about staying any longer because he knew it meant the bill would be on me since he did not nor could he get a job at this point.

I found out that this very thing was happening all over the United States. Even in Connecticut on the front pages of newspapers there were psychiatric doctors pleading to be heard as they went in front of the board of insurances and courts. The doctor's wanted to be heard for their patients. The patients needed more time in the hospital to be stabilized before kicking them out into the streets. This particular doctor was actually muzzled by the courts. Money should not be the driving force of such a serious situation. So I knew this was a giant perplexing problem all across our nation.

I began wondering…isn't there some way we could all be happy? Why couldn't the cooperation promise to stay with the same insurance for five years? This way the insurance companies would get their money back because the patients would not be in and out of the hospital as much. The patient would be more stabilized and would have the same doctor for trust level, which is what they desperately need. Most of all, the patients would get the help that they need to carry on a more productive and meaningful life. This way the doctors who know the patients best would have more say than the dictation of a distant third party—the insurance party.

Who knows, maybe my husband could have had the help he so desperately needed if his doctor had a chance to help James without so much pressure from the insurance people to get him out of the hospital before he really should have left his care.

The Road Marked... Life Goes On

James 1:2–12

Consider it pure joy, my brothers, whenever you face trials of many kinds, because you know that the testing of your faith develops perseverance. Perseverance must finish its work so that you may be mature and complete, not lacking anything. If any of you lacks wisdom, he should ask God, who gives generously to all without finding fault, and it will be given to him. But when he asks, he must believe and not doubt, because he who doubts is like a wave of the sea, blown and tossed by the wind,. That man should not think he will receive anything from the Lord; he is a double-minded man, unstable in all he does. The brother in humble circumstances ought to take pride in his high position. But the one who is rich should take pride in his low position, because he will pass away like a wild flower. For the sun rises with scorching heat and withers the plant; its blossom falls and its beauty is destroyed. In the same way, the rich man will fade away

EVEN WHILE HE GOES ABOUT HIS BUSINESS. BLESSED IS THE MAN WHO PERSEVERES UNDER TRIAL, BECAUSE WHEN HE HAS STOOD THE TEST, HE WILL RECEIVE THE CROWN OF LIFE THAT GOD HAD PROMISED TO THOSE WHO LOVE HIM.

It is inevitable that trials will come in our lives. Some people turn to philosophers, some harbor hurt, some harbor anger. Christians are to look to God's Word. Various trials come in different sizes, spread out in time, different colors; they are costumed designed just for us. They even come without warning. God's Word tells us they have a purpose. They are to stretch us spiritually. We are to become mature, enduring, and reasoning individuals.

My daughter Kristi wrote a passage with great meaning when she was in high school, which said it in a different format. She even drew a picture to emphasis its meaning. It read, "To get through anger *you* must pass through the hurt. To get to sadness *you* must understand the hurt. Through prayer and dedication *you* can achieve all goals."

God understands all hurts. His Son died for us. The basic fiber of who He is has been there, is there, and will be there. There is no hurt that He cannot understand because He had it happen to Him over 2000 years ago. He also is there when it happens to us. We are an integral part of each other. The trials we go through, whether abandonment, verbal abuse, sexual abuse, authoritative abuse, volatile abuse, terrorism, or even life itself has no touch on the fiber of the soul, if we only trust Him as our Lord and Savior.

God's people that are born again have a connection to the purpose of our very being. Even though it may be a difficult pathway, we have been given or taken by our own free will; He knows there is a way out to freedom. And all along the way has not been in vain if we turn it over to Him. He will take it to higher grounds than we know. Step by step we must turn it over to Him.

You know it is quite interesting how God's truth sets us free. A few weeks ago I went to a secular seminar for health professionals called "Self-Destructive Emotions." It was given by Nick Hall, Ph.D. He is well known around the world for his understanding of how emotions affect our wellbeing. In his seminar he had over 123 references that were a result of years of scientific study along with his many years of experience. He even told me to use whatever I needed to write this book. A few points I wish to convey that he said were of the area of *contentment*. He stated that there were two kinds of thoughts on religious prayers. One being a religion-ritualistic and the other spiritual—a deep meaning intrinsic kind, the one that says, "Thy will be done." Interesting enough this is found in Matthew 6:9–10. This is where Jesus was praying the "Lord's Prayer." "Our Father is heaven, hallowed be your name, your kingdom come, *your will be done* on earth as it is in heaven." Others found in the Bible are as follows; "I desire to do *your will...*"found in Psalm 40:8; "teach me to do *your will...*" found in Psalm 143:10; "not as I will, but as *you will...*" Matthew 26:39; "If anyone chooses to do *God's will...*" John 7:17; "For I have not hesitated to proclaim to you the whole will of God..."

Acts 20:27; "...to test and approve what *God's will* is—his good, pleasing and *perfect will...*" Romans 12:2; "Therefore do not be foolish, but understand what the *Lord's will is...*" Ephesians 5:17; "...for it is God who works in you *to will* and to act according to his good purpose" Philippians 2:13; "...give thanks in all circumstances, for this is *God's will* for you in Christ Jesus," 1 Thessalonians 5:18 and there are many other verses that speak to *thy will be done.*

According to Hill, he said the other area of true (pure) happiness is when we are *contended* with whatever we have. Once again there it is in God's Word—Philippians 4:11–13. Paul is writing to the Christians in Philippi "...for I have learned to be *content* whatever the circumstances. I know what it is to be in need, and I know what it is to have plenty. I have learned the secret of being content in any and every situation, whether well fed or hungry, whether living in plenty or in want. I can do everything through him who gives me strength." But godliness with *contentment* is great gain. For we brought nothing into the world, and we can take nothing out of it. But if we have food and clothing, we will be *content* with that, 1 Timothy 6:6–8; "... be *content* with what you have..." Hebrews 13: 5, again there are others in God's Word about contentment.

The answers are true, and the power to live them out is in Him and Him alone.

In reading the book by Elizabeth George, *Loving God With All Your Mind*, she writes about the "what ifs" and "if only." She says, "If only thoughts about the past can rob us of peace and joy in the present. Philippians 4:8—to think or "whatever things are true (or real) comes to our rescue concerning our thoughts of the past. That's because the past is no more real than the future."

My God is the God of the past, the present, and the future! He has promised to guide you throughout your life too, and receive you to glory afterward, Psalm 73:24. As David said in Psalm 23:6 "Surely goodness and mercy shall follow me all the days of my life, and I will dwell in the house of the Lord forever."

Through all of my children's experiences with their Dad, my prayer is that God will bring peace. My prayers for my children and their mates are that they not be a follower but a leader of people into His Kingdom and knowing with complete understanding of their authority in Jesus yet with the balance of having a submissive and humble spirit. I also pray for them daily that they will grow daily in the fruit of the spirit, which is love, joy, peace, patience, kindness, goodness, faithfulness, gentleness, and self-control. Galatians 5:22. Life does go on, and I pray that we will all be contented in doing His purpose, His will in our lives for something that is far more than this earth could possibly give and bring others to the saving knowledge of Him.

The Road of Remembrance

Psalm 146:5–7

Blessed is he whose help is the God of Jacob, whose hope is the Lord his God, the Maker of heaven and earth, the sea, and everything in them-the Lord, who remains faithful forever.

After a few months went by, I decided to paint my house from inside out. Since it was wintertime, I began inside first. I went to the store to get just the right paint color. After three months I finished nine rooms and touch ups with trim work on three other rooms. During this time I had much time to reflect. Now that the house was to myself with my mom passing away in March, my sister getting married and moving in June to California, Stephanie in Dallas for schooling, my other two children already married, and James passing away that October, it was quite quiet to say the least.

I have some Willow Tree Angels that I have been collecting for several years with the help of my children, family, and friends. I was dusting off the mantel area after I had painted the walls. I was painstaking, placing them just right on the mantel, looking at each angel's given purpose, when suddenly my mind went back to my childhood. One is Angel of Light, another Angel of Hope, Angel of Prayer, Angel of Serenity, Angel of Love, etc. I reflected over an hour on stories that were so special to me of my childhood, like the Angel of Learning. I remember so clearly how my dad's immense thirst for truth. His reading for hours at a time even at age eighty-three and his interest in life was just unbelievable to conceive. The warm times we bonded together on Sunday afternoons reading missionary books on his lap I remembered. The encyclopedias he opened up daily to read up on a topic and the daily newspapers, auto-biographies, combined into endless hours of reading. The Angel of Miracles reminded me of when my mom let one of our cats have her baby kittens inside our house's desk drawers so we could see the miracle being born before our young eyes. The stories went on and on until I came to the last of the angels I placed in the center. It was the Angel of Remembrance that my friend Barbara gave to me at James' memorial. Suddenly as if God himself were standing there, an over whelming sense of God's presence came over me. God had seen it all, He has orchestrated the whole happenings of my life. He had been there right from the beginning. I sat down on my loveseat and cried and cried. He gave me that background to give me the fortitude to go through the trials for my future with James' illness. James really gave me the pull like an old farm hand pump. It takes the force of the pressure I needed to grow in faith and go to tell others of His great love and mercy He has for us.

He is the one who controlled my life in the past and controls it in the present and into the future! In Psalms 77:13 it says: Your ways, O God, are holy. What god is so great as our God? Our faith in God is strengthened when we recall how God brings us through trials, how He taught us on the mountain and in the valleys of life." It is no wonder my mom and dad's favorite hymn was "Great is Thy Faithfulness" "...morning to morning new mercies I see. All I have needed Thy hand has provided, great is Thy faithfulness Lord unto me."

As Elizabeth George said in her book, "By His transforming power, God will redeem even the worst, the most painful, and the most perplexing aspects of your past. In fact, some of the saints I know who graciously and continually extend God's gentleness, peace, and encouragement to others are those who have tasted pain. God, in His goodness and power, has used their experiences to make them more Christ-like, and He is truly glorified in their lives."

These trails only come to open a way for us to grow into a total dependence on Him. He enabled me to deal with the circumstances and the stress. His grace was sufficient and because of it, my spiritual growth did occur in my life. I know more of who God is because of it. The waiting, trusting, and persevering caused my faith to grow in God. Hopefully, I can become more effective in relating to people and their difficulties.

I really like what Elizabeth George says about existing vs. serving. "It's true that difficult and painful circumstances can make it difficult for us to pursue excellence as we serve God. But circumstances that are *too comfortable* can have the same effect. We can become people who merely *exist* rather than ones who actively *serve* God. Content with where we are, we fail to press forward toward Christ-like maturity."

Romans 8:28 tells us, "And we know that in all things God works for the good of those who love him, who have been called according to his purpose." Isaiah 55:8–9 reads, "For my thoughts are not your thoughts, neither are your ways my ways, declares the Lord. As the heavens are higher than the earth, so are my ways higher than your ways and my thoughts than your thoughts." God's good purpose is hard to understand sometimes, but when you think of a high tower looking down, it is a totally different perspective on life. That is what He is to us—the high tower. He sees things from the past, present, and future. This is when one loves God with all their mind, heart, and soul; we need to trust God for the ultimate purpose.

I agree with Elizabeth George as she writes, "He is working it all out for good. His plan reflects His purpose, His methods, and His timetable…not ours. And never forget that while God is working out His plan in your life, painful as it may be at times, you are becoming His *masterpiece*! One reason many of us fail to enjoy the adventure of the Christian life is because it is a process. We like the end results more than we like the process that gets us there. But between today and the good end that God promises, we have to go through a process." It is much like the form of a butterfly's process of becoming one. If we tried to help it along, it would not be the right timing, we would ruin its purpose, its life, its beauty, its freedom.

Elizabeth brings one more concept in her book that I would like to share with you about looking through the eyes of an artist. "As the story goes, one day a colossal cube of marble was delivered to Michelangelo's art studio. He walked around it several times, at first surveying it from a step back, then looking at it closely. He touched it with his hands and even pressed his face against the cold block of stone. Suddenly he grabbed a mallet and a chisel and swung mightily. Blow after blow caused small chips of marble as well as large chunks to fly in every direction.

Watching in awe, his apprentice screamed above the noise of shattering stone." What are you doing? You are ruining a perfect piece of marble!"

With the passion of an artist with a vision, Michelangelo answered, "I see an angel in there, and I've got to get him out!"

A.W. Tozer recaps how God is always working in our lives. By God's grace, you and I can better accept every event in our lives when we realize that *all* of the details and elements of our lives are in the hands of our infinitely wise God who knows us and loves us as no one else does. This perfect wisdom calls us to faith. The testimony of faith is that no matter how things look in this fallen world, all God's acts are wrought in perfect wisdom.

Although God's ways are often mysterious, by faith we believe in the infinite and holy wisdom behind them. By faith we trust in the wisdom of God that stands behind the events we don't understand. As Oswald Chambers points out, "Trustfulness is based on confidence in God whose ways I do not understand; if I did, there would be no need for trust."

My Road is to Praise Him

Romans 11: 33–36

Oh, the depth of the riches of the wisdom and knowledge of God! How unsearchable his judgments, and his paths beyond tracing out! Who has known the mind of the Lord? Or who has been his counselor? Who has ever given to God, that God should repay him? For from him and through him and to him are all things. To him be the glory forever! Amen.

Did you know that there are over 300 names for God? They are names He named himself—they are his attributes. One song I so much love to listen to because it brings just a little insight to who He is. Not that any one song or songs could contain who He is. I feel much like when Solomon, in his entire royal splendor such as no king over Israel ever had before, wrote about the magnificent temple he made for God. In 2 Chronicles 6:18b, "The heavens, even the highest heavens, cannot contain you. How much less this temple I have built!"

The song is called, "Lord, You're Holy;" words and music by Eddie James.

> Lord, You're holy, Lord, You're holy and we lift You up and magnify Your name. I look around and I see all the works your hands have made; The awesomeness of You and how Your love will never fade. Mere words cannot express how I feel inside, and I can't decide Your glory divine. But as a token of my love. That is what I'll do. I'll lift my hands and cry. There are not enough words that I can say to tell You how much I appreciate all the wonderful things You've given me. Your loving kindness, Your tender mercy. It's my desire to praise You, and tell you how much I love You. You're worthy of all the glory, and You're worthy of all the praise. But I don't know why You would love me, why You would show me so much mercy, why You would suffer and die for me way back at Calvary. I thank You, Jesus. I thank You, Jesus. I thank You, I'm thankin You, Jesus. You're worthy of all the praise You are Wonderful, glorious, holy and righteous, Victorious, Conqueror, triumphant and Mighty! Healer, Deliver, Shield and Defense, Strong Tower and my best Friend, Omnipotent, Omnipresent, Soon Coming King! Alpha, Omega, Lord of everything! Holy, Holy, Holy is Your name. Holy, Holy, Holy is Your name! Your name Your name!

Jewel and Dale Erickson are two of our dear missionary friends from England. In her sympathy card to the family, Jewel wrote with such meaningful and sensitive compassion,

> We were so sad to read the e-mail from Stephanie informing us of James' death. Stephanie, you were so wise in saying that God could have once again inter-

> vened, but this time He decided to allow your dad to end his misery. Though bipolar disease is a mystery to us, we know it is no mystery to our Lord, who is full of grace and mercy. As time passes, we pray that you will remember James not as he was in the grip of his disease but rather as the outgoing, loving, creative, dynamic personality that was the real man. In the end may you be left with memories of the good times you shared and the love that will always be a part of you... May God's steadfast love be your strength and your hope as He carries you to a place of peace.

My belief is that God has chosen in his sovereign will to use this story by His redemptive force to generate thoughts, feelings, and beliefs to point to Him for our answers in life. First Peter 1:3–9 says, "Blessed be the God and Father of our Lord Jesus Christ. According to His great mercy, He has given us a new birth into a living hope through the resurrection of Jesus Christ from the dead, and into an inheritance that is imperishable, uncorrupt, and unfading, kept in heaven for you, who are being protected by God's power through faith for a salvation that is ready to be revealed in the last time. You rejoice in this, though now for a short time you have had to be distressed by various trials so that the genuineness of your faith—more valuable than gold, which perishes though refined by fire—may result in praise, glory, and honor at the revelation of Jesus Christ. You love Him though you have not seen Him. And though not seeing Him now, you believe in Him and rejoice with inexpressible and glorious joy because you are receiving the goal of your faith, the salvation of your souls."

My desire in writing this book is to bring you, the reader, to the place of peace. If you do not know Him, our precious Lord, you may by simply asking Him into your life.

Right now you can ask God to enter your life. You can do this through prayer. Prayer means talking honestly with God. At this moment you can call out to God by telling Him something like this in sincerity:

"God, I have turned away from You in my heart, but I want to change that. I want to know You. I want to receive Jesus Christ and His forgiveness into my life. I don't want to be separated from You anymore. Be the God of my life from this day onward. Thank you, God."

Have you just now sincerely asked God into your life? If you have, you have a lot to look forward to. God promises to make your present life one of greater satisfaction through knowing Him.[26] Where is God? He promises to make His home in you.[27] And He gives you eternal life.[28]

No matter what happens in the world around you, God can be there for you. Though people do not follow God's ways, God is able to take horrible circumstances and bring about His plan anyway. God is ultimately in control over world events. If you are God's, then you can rest on the promise that, "All things work together for good for those who love God and are called according to His purpose."[29]

Jesus Christ said, "My peace I give to you; not as the world gives, do I give to you. Let not your heart be troubled. In the world you have tribulation, but take courage; I have overcome the world."[30] He promises never to fail us or forsake us.[31]

To grow in your knowledge of God and His will for your life, read the sections Matthew, Mark, Luke, and John in the Bible.

(26) John 10:10
(27) John 14:23
(28) 1 John 5:11–13
(29) Romans 8:28
(30) John 14:27 and 16:33
(31) Hebrews 13:5

Our other missionary friends in England are Roger and Donna Vann, and they have put together, along with other missionaries, an interactive Web site to learn more about Jesus and the knowledge of who God is.

Consider several websites with questions and answers about life when wondering *Where is God in the midst of tragedy?* www.gotquestions.org or www.lookingfor-god.com

My hope and prayer for you is that as I have shared my story, you have been lead from your home to the road that is everlasting. As you walk- love the light that leads you from darkness into a purposeful, peaceful, and secure future, and may God richly bless you on your road of pursuit to true happiness and fulfillment. In Proverbs 13:4B it says, "...but the desires of the diligent are fully satisfied." As you walk diligently toward Him, know God is with you lovingly leading you on your road to Him.

Behavioral Science Viewpoint

Written by Kristi Brady Yetter—
B.S. degree in Psychology

According to the Diagnostic and Statistical Manual of Mental Disorders—fourth edition (DSM-IV ™) "the essential feature of borderline personality disorder is a pervasive pattern of instability of interpersonal relationships, self-image, and affects, and marked impulsivity that begins by early adulthood and is present in a variety of contexts" (p. 650). Together the definition is complex and difficult to understand, but when your life is surrounded by each "pattern" you begin to understand the complexities as an understanding of the individual.

"Individuals with borderline personality disorder make frantic efforts to avoid real or imagined abandonment" (p. 650). My father, as a young child, would unknowingly shift the feelings of abandonment from his childhood, from consciousness to unconscious. Transferring the feeling to the unconscious would allow him to avoid the uncomfortable feelings in hope to avoid his true feelings of anxiety of real abandonment.

"The perception of impending separation or rejection, or the loss of external structure, can lead to profound changes in self-image, affect, cognition, and behavior. These individuals are very sensitive to environmental circumstances" (p. 650). When jobs would fluctuate from yearly to monthly because of an impending issue that arose in the work environment, it was very clear that it internally troubled him. He would fight for the underdog and would become irate when someone would say something uncalled for or treat another person in a negative manner. His thoughts were "treat others as you would want to be treated," but his views were often an exaggeration of what actually occurred. He blamed the external environment, as he got older the fight in him didn't fade, but the internal strength that he once had later became outward and forthcoming. He personally would feel that the individual was rejecting him as a person and felt the need to correct *their* misguided thoughts. His cognitive understanding would become misguided and would affect his behavior and cause his external environment to become one of disarray.

"Individuals with borderline personality disorder have a pattern of unstable and intense relationships" there were many intense relationships that my father was involved in. Dr. Dot was an aggressive man who only thought of himself and never others. He led my father down a path of destruction, which in the end cost him his job. "There are sudden and dramatic shifts in self-image, characterized by shifting goals, values, and vocational aspirations" (p. 651).

"Individuals with the disorder display impulsivity in at least two areas that are potentially self-damaging" (p. 651). As read in the book, my father displayed many of the acts: spending money in an irresponsible manner, driving recklessly, and binge eating. His binges were what he called fasting. Before my father passed, he was on one of his kicks of fasting. I came over with my husband and found the refrigerator to be empty and when I asked what he was eating, he pulled out an old chicken and said that he was just fine. I went shopping for him after talking with my mother about the situation and later found out he gave the food to a shelter. My mother mentioned the reckless driving and the continual misguidance he had with handling money.

"Individuals with Borderline Personality Disorder may display affective instability that is due to a marked reactivity of moods...periods of anger, panic, or despair" (p. 651). Mood swings were common with my father he would never have a moment where he would be content and be okay with being content. There was always something bigger and better to be caught. "Easily bored and seeking something to do." They may display extreme sarcasm, enduring bitterness, or verbal outbursts (p. 651). Although my father was fun and adventurous, he could be quit embarrassing to his family. His jokes were many times crude and uncalled for. He had many verbal outbursts that would cause unwanted attention and it would not faze him in the slightest.

To better describe some of the patterns, "A Manic Episode is defined by a distinct period during which there is an abnormally and persistently elevated, expansive, or irritable mood" (p. 328). It was as though he craved the "high" per say. He would not just jump from one extreme to another; it would take time to reach a manic episode, which I believe was the hardest thing to diagnose. However, eventually he would reach the peak, and what peaks must have an opportunity to balance out. Basically what I am trying to say is a manic episode was followed by a depressive state, which would eventually take my father's life. "This period of abnormal mood must last at least one week" (or less if hospitalization is required). As the episode crept up to a full manic episode, there were the following symptoms that often accompanied the episode: "...inflated self-esteem or grandiosity, decreased need for sleep, flight of ideas, distractibility..." (p. 328).

"Individuals with a Manic Episode frequently do not recognize that they are ill and resist efforts to be treated. They may travel impulsively to other cities, losing contact with relatives and caretakers" (p. 330). I can't say that my father ever resisted seeking help, but I know he thought he could get off the medication because he was healed. The constant battle he had must have been such a struggle for him. I cannot begin to imagine the frustration he must have had while taking the medication. The constant struggle and thinking about meds he was put on would someday be an ending to the illness.

There were many close friends that did not realize that my father had a disorder and thought that James was merely eccentric at times, but he had a great heart. I can attest, he did have a big heart for people and wanted all three of his children to be all that they could be. He gave all three children what he could. We did have our many ups and downs with financial needs, but God was always there to insure that we were not left unfed.

American Psychiatric Association (1994) *Diagnostic and Statistical Manual of Mental Disorders* 4th edition DSM-IV. Washington D.C.

There are three things that remain: faith, hope, and love, and the greatest of these is love. 1 Corinthians 13:13

Love Transcends

Time is limited because time has boundaries.
On earth we too are surrounded by limitations.
But
There is one force of life that transcends time.
Comfort and peace are wrapped in this one timeless word,

Love.
Love is eternal because God is Love.

It is ancient but ever new.
Empowered by need, it gives strength beyond human understanding.
Loved ones feel it while on earth.

One day,
life as we know it,
ends
as dear ones leave us for their eternal home.
But the thought of love shared, warms the hearts of those who are left.

Life on earth is temporal.
Love is eternal.

Love
transcends time.

—Janice McCament

CPSIA information can be obtained at www.ICGtesting.com
Printed in the USA
LVOW08s1045070716

495161LV00001B/2/P

9 781617 396601